T0214817

Lecture Notes in Computer Science 10560

Commenced Publication in 1973
Founding and Former Series Editors:
Gerhard Goos, Juris Hartmanis, and Jan van Leeuwen

More information about this series at http://www.springer.com/series/8183

Marina L. Gavrilova · C.J. Kenneth Tan
Alexei Sourin (Eds.)

Transactions on Computational Science XXX

Special Issue on Cyberworlds and Cybersecurity

Springer

Editors-in-Chief

Marina L. Gavrilova
University of Calgary
Calgary, AB
Canada

C.J. Kenneth Tan
Sardina Systems
Tallinn
Estonia

Guest Editor

Alexei Sourin
Nanyang Technological University
Singapore
Singapore

ISSN 0302-9743   ISSN 1611-3349   (electronic)
Lecture Notes in Computer Science
ISSN 1866-4733   ISSN 1866-4741   (electronic)
Transactions on Computational Science
ISBN 978-3-662-56005-1   ISBN 978-3-662-56006-8   (eBook)
https://doi.org/10.1007/978-3-662-56006-8

Library of Congress Control Number: 2017957821

Printed on acid-free paper

This Springer imprint is published by Springer Nature
The registered company is Springer-Verlag GmbH Germany
The registered company address is: Heidelberger Platz 3, 14197 Berlin, Germany

LNCS Transactions on Computational Science

Computational science, an emerging and increasingly vital field, is now widely recognized as an integral part of scientific and technical investigations, affecting researchers and practitioners in areas ranging from aerospace and automotive research to biochemistry, electronics, geosciences, mathematics, and physics. Computer systems research and the exploitation of applied research naturally complement each other. The increased complexity of many challenges in computational science demands the use of supercomputing, parallel processing, sophisticated algorithms, and advanced system software and architecture. It is therefore invaluable to have input by systems research experts in applied computational science research.

Transactions on Computational Science focuses on original high-quality research in the realm of computational science in parallel and distributed environments, also encompassing the underlying theoretical foundations and the applications of large-scale computation.

The journal offers practitioners and researchers the opportunity to share computational techniques and solutions in this area, to identify new issues, and to shape future directions for research, and it enables industrial users to apply leading-edge, large-scale, high-performance computational methods.

In addition to addressing various research and application issues, the journal aims to present material that is validated – crucial to the application and advancement of the research conducted in academic and industrial settings. In this spirit, the journal focuses on publications that present results and computational techniques that are verifiable.

Scope

The scope of the journal includes, but is not limited to, the following computational methods and applications:

- Aeronautics and Aerospace
- Astrophysics
- Big Data Analytics
- Bioinformatics
- Biometric Technologies
- Climate and Weather Modeling
- Communication and Data Networks
- Compilers and Operating Systems
- Computer Graphics
- Computational Biology
- Computational Chemistry
- Computational Finance and Econometrics

- Computational Fluid Dynamics
- Computational Geometry
- Computational Number Theory
- Data Representation and Storage
- Data Mining and Data Warehousing
- Information and Online Security
- Grid Computing
- Hardware/Software Co-design
- High-Performance Computing
- Image and Video Processing
- Information Systems
- Information Retrieval
- Modeling and Simulations
- Mobile Computing
- Numerical and Scientific Computing
- Parallel and Distributed Computing
- Robotics and Navigation
- Supercomputing
- System-on-Chip Design and Engineering
- Virtual Reality and Cyberworlds
- Visualization

Editorial

The Transactions on Computational Science journal is part of the Springer series *Lecture Notes in Computer Science*, and is devoted to the range of computational science issues, from theoretical aspects to application-dependent studies and the validation of emerging technologies.

The journal focuses on original high-quality research in the realm of computational science in parallel and distributed environments, encompassing the theoretical foundations and the applications of large-scale computations and massive data processing. Practitioners and researchers share computational techniques and solutions in the area, identify new issues, and shape future directions for research, as well as enable industrial users to apply the techniques presented.

The current volume is devoted to state-of-the-art approaches in the domain of cybersecurity and virtual worlds. It is comprised of the extended versions of the best papers presented at the International Conference on Cyberworlds, held in Chongqing, China, September 28–30, 2016. The first paper is a position paper by one of the Editors-in-Chief of the journal, outlining emerging directions of research at the intersection of two important domains: cybersecurity and cyberworlds, specifically focusing on mining behavioral data from online social networks. The other five full papers are extended versions of selected conference papers. They cover topics such as: privacy assurance in online location services, recognizing human gait using KINECT sensors, hand gesture recognition for computer games, scene matching between the source image and the target image for virtual reality applications, and human identification using brain-waves.

We would like to extend our sincere appreciation to Special Issue Guest Editor, Associate Prof. Alexei Sourin, NTU, Singapore, for his dedication to the special issue. We thank all the reviewers for their work on this special issue. We would also like to thank all of the authors for submitting their papers to the journal and the associate editors for their valuable work.

It is our hope that the collection of six articles presented in this issue will be a valuable resource for Transactions on Computational Science readers and will stimulate further research into the key area of virtual worlds and online security.

July 2017

Marina L. Gavrilova
C.J. Kenneth Tan

Guest Editor's Preface

Special Issue on Cyberworlds 2016

This special issue includes the extended versions of five papers selected from the papers presented at the 2016 International Conference on Cyberworlds, which was held in Chongqing, China, September 28–30, 2016 (http://www3.ntu.edu.sg/home/assourin/cw/cw2016). The International Conferences on Cyberworlds (http://www.cyberworlds-conference.org) have been organized annually since 2002. The conferences are focused on networked and shared virtual worlds, virtual collaborative spaces, shape modeling, virtual humans and avatars, multimodal interaction and rendering, computer vision for augmented and mixed reality, cognitive informatics, brain-computer interfaces, affective computing, social computing, online communities, e-learning, multi-user web games, art and heritage in cyberspace, cyber-museums, cyberethics and cyberlaws, cybersecurity, welfare in cyberspace, data mining and warehousing in cyberspace, and visual analytics. The five selected papers included in this transactions volume reflect the great diversity of the topics covered by Cyberworlds 2016 as well as the excellent level of its scientific contributions.

The first paper, "KINECT Face Recognition Using Occluded Area Localization Method" by Fatema Tuz Zohra and Marina Gavrilova, proposes a new face recognition technique that takes into account partial occlusion, while still accurately identifying the user. The occluded facial areas are detected from the Kinect depth images by extracting features using Uniform Local Binary Patterns. For localizing occluded regions from the Kinect depth images, a threshold-based approach is used to identify the areas close to the camera. The recognition system discards the occluded regions of the facial images and matches only the non-occluded facial part with the gallery of images to find the best possible match. The performance of the recognition system has been tested on the EUROKOM Kinect face database containing different types of occluded and non-occluded faces with neutral expressions.

The second paper, "Scene-Aware Style Transferring Using GIST" by Masahiro Toyoura, Noriyuki Abe, and Xiaoyang Mao, proposes a new method of transferring style between images by considering scene matching between the source image and the target image. Artists often employ different colors and brushwork for individual subjects. Likewise, the connections between various subjects in a work also affect the colors and brushwork used. The proposed method begins with input images, searches an example database for paintings with scenes similar to that in the input image, and transfers the color and brushwork of the paintings to the corresponding target images to generate painterly images that reflect specific styles. The proposed method applies a GIST approach to the process of searching for paintings with similar scenes before performing style transfers. The spatial correspondence between the source image and the target image is also used to ensure close correlation between various elements in order to reproduce styles faithfully.

The third paper, "Privacy-Preserved Spatial Skyline Queries in Location-Based Services" by Rong Tan and Wen Si, introduces the privacy-preserved spatial skyline query where the distances calculated between the query points and the objects change from 'point to point' to 'region to point'. It is the first effort to process relative skyline queries based on a 'region to point' method. The authors propose three approaches: a straightforward method, and two methods manipulating the properties of Voronoi diagrams and Network Voronoi diagrams for the Euclidean space and road-network situations, respectively. Furthermore, with respect to the changes of query conditions, another two algorithms to dynamically update the results were proposed so that the heavy re-calculation could be avoided. The empirical experiments show that the proposed approaches exhibit good performance in retrieving the skyline points of a privacy-preserved spatial skyline query.

The fourth paper, "Comparison Analysis of Overt and Covert Mental Stimuli of Brain Signal for Person Identification" by Md Wasiur Rahman and Marina Gavrilova, describes the development of an EEG-based biometric security system. The purpose of this research is to find the relationship between thinking capability and person identification accuracy by comparison analyzing of overt and covert mental stimuli of brain signals. The Discrete Wavelet Transform is used to extract different significant features which separate alpha, beta, and theta bands of frequencies of the EEG signal. Extracted EEG features of different bands and their combinations such as alpha-beta, alpha-theta, theta-beta, alpha-beta-theta are classified using an artificial neural network trained with the back propagation algorithm. Another classifier K-nearest neighbors is used to verify the results of this experiment. Both classification results show that the alpha band has a higher convergence rate than other bands, beta and theta, for the overt EEG signal. From overt mental stimuli, the authors also discovered that individual bands provide better performance than band combination.

The fifth paper, "The Man-Machine Finger-Guessing Game Based on Cooperation Mechanism" by Xiaoyan Zhou, Zhiquan Feng, Yu Qiao, Xue Fan, and Xiaohui Yang, describes the design of a man-machine finger-guessing game based on the IntelliSense and man-machine coordination mechanism of hand gesture. The image sequence is obtained by the Kinect sensor and the human hand is extracted using segmentation and skin color modeling. The proposed shape context density distribution Feature, which combines the density distribution feature algorithm and the shape context recognition algorithm, is used to extract gesture identity. The gestures are finally identified by registering with templates in the pre-established gesture library. The paper also proposes a new human-computer cooperative mechanism.

The conference organizers are deeply grateful to *Transactions on Computational Science* Editor-in-Chief, Prof. Marina Gavrilova, and the journal Editorial staff for their continuing help and assistance during the whole process of preparation of these papers. We also wish to thank the authors for their high-quality contributions and their great cooperation in preparing this special issue.

Alexei Sourin

LNCS Transactions on Computational Science – Editorial Board

Contents

Emerging Directions in Virtual Worlds and Biometric Security Research   1
　Marina L. Gavrilova

KINECT Face Recognition Using Occluded Area Localization Method   12
　Fatema Tuz Zohra and Marina Gavrilova

Scene-Aware Style Transferring Using GIST   29
　Masahiro Toyoura, Noriyuki Abe, and Xiaoyang Mao

Privacy-Preserved Spatial Skyline Queries in Location-Based Services.   50
　Rong Tan and Wen Si

Comparison Analysis of Overt and Covert Mental Stimuli
of Brain Signal for Person Identification   73
　Md Wasiur Rahman and Marina Gavrilova

The Man-Machine Finger-Guessing Game Based
on Cooperation Mechanism   92
　Xiaoyan Zhou, Zhiquan Feng, Yu Qiao, Xue Fan,
　and Xiaohui Yang

Author Index   111

Emerging Directions in Virtual Worlds and Biometric Security Research

Marina L. Gavrilova$^{(\boxtimes)}$

Biometric Technologies Lab, Department of Computer Science,
University of Calgary, Calgary, Canada
marina@cpsc.ucalgary.ca

Abstract. Recent research in the areas of computer graphics, virtual reality and cyberworlds is increasingly concerned with the security applications. In the area of cyberworlds, human features such as faces, hair, walking patterns, voice, behaviour and a manner of communications are being simulated and studied. Moreover, research into social online interactions, and an effort to mimic those interactions and appearances through virtual humans and robots has become abundant. This position paper discusses the state-of-the-art research in the fields of biometric recognition, multi-modal and cancelable biometrics, artificial biometrics and social behavioral studies conducted in the Biometric Technologies laboratory at the University of Calgary, Canada. Social behavioral pattern analysis is the emerging domain in the biometric recognition; the idea behind it is to extract behavioral clues from the everyday human interactions. Activity-related biometric authentication provides an unobtrusive and natural alternative for physiological biometric that can exploit everyday life activities involving interaction with objects or people for extracting biometric signature. Recent research demonstrated that it is possible to extract the behavioral traits not only from traditional behavioral identifiers, such as voice, gait or signature, but also from an online interactions of users or an editing behavior of Wikipedia article authors. An overview of this emerging areas of research that brings virtual worlds modeling and biometric security recognition fields together has been presented at DRDC 2017 National Defense and Security Workshop, Canada. This Editor-in-Chief Position paper is based on the results discussed there as well as on the report submitted to DRDC following the workshop (Gavrilova 2017).

Keywords: Information security · Cyberworlds · Online social networks · Machine learning · Social biometrics · Behavioral biometrics

1 Introduction

Over the past decade, computational sciences research has evolved from theory-based fundamental studies focused on enhancing the recognition performance into a dynamic, multi-disciplinary field that spans areas of big data analytics, cognitive computing, cyberworlds, machine learning and information visualization. From formal methodologies that describe phenomena happening in a real world, to virtual avatar recognition in cyberworlds, it has broaden its scope significantly. New discoveries find

M.L. Gavrilova et al. (Eds.): Trans. on Comput. Sci. XXX, LNCS 10560, pp. 1–11, 2017.
https://doi.org/10.1007/978-3-662-56006-8_1

applications in such areas as psychology, neurosciences, medicine, virtual reality, games, decision making and social interactions. Traditional definition of biometrics recognition system includes the notion of recognizing someone's identity from a collected biometric data (Jain et al. 2004). This data typically includes physiological, behavioural, soft, and a recently introduced social traits (Gavrilova and Monwar 2013). Physiological biometrics such as face, iris, retina, ear, and a fingerprint can be captured by a specialized devices, which now include not only traditional cameras and video/audio recorders, but a new generation of infrared sensors, odour sensors, gait recording devices, remote vital sign measuring devices, and even Kinect motion capturing consumer grade product (Chew et al. 2012, Li et al. 2013). Behavioural characteristics, which include the way a person walks (gait), the way a person talks (voice), the way a person writes (typing patterns, keystroke pressure), or the way a person authenticates documents (signature), can be obtained from the same of other sensors (Barakova et al. 2015). Soft biometrics typically represent easily observed but not a highly unique data. Gender, height, weight, age, colour of eyes or a hair constitute soft biometrics. A good biometric trait should typically contain four attributes: universality, distinctiveness, permanence, and collectability to become a biometric identifier (Jain et al. 2004).

Recently, scientists started to pay attention to the way how humans interact socially with each other. A social behavioural biometric (or social biometric) was proposed as a new way to obtain supplementary but sometimes crucial for authentication information (Sultana et al. 2017a, Sultana et al. 2017b). In such a system, the social behavioural features are extracted from the way users interact through various social on-line and off-line networks. This includes user's online presence patterns (time, day, month), the nature of interaction (tweets, blogs, chats), the content of interaction (topics, likes, opinions), online game playing strategies, virtual world avatar preferences, etc. (Sultana et al. 2014a, Sultana et al. 2015b). One of the main features, which is crucial for research on the social behavioural biometrics, is the communication patterns in the networks of users and the composition of such networks themselves. It is generating a lot of interest and getting traction in biometric research, as well as in related fields looking into human interaction, physiological studies, user profiling, pattern recognition, authorship identification, and collective intelligence (Sultana et al. 2014a, Gavrilova and Yampolskiy 2011). The idea can be transferred to a real world as well. For instance, in a given social context some social behavioural patterns such as friends and acquaintances, daily routine, psychological states, style of conversation, gestures and emotions during conversations, preferences, spatial information, and activity logs can play important role in recognizing a person. Such patterns can also provide a unique set of tools to promote better understanding of collaborative processes, workflow dynamics and risk analysis in collaborative/social environments in real and virtual worlds (Gavrilova et al. 2016, Wang et al. 2016).

This position paper investigates how existing biometric multi-modal systems can be advanced by integrating social behavioural information. Extensive discussions on how the social behavioural biometrics can be extracted and applied in various security and authentication applications are presented. In addition, the paper compares social aesthetic biometrics with soft biometrics, and discusses the notion of ArtiMetrics –or Artificial Biometrics, in the context of mutli-modal biometric research. The work is concluded with some insights onto current and emerging research in biometric domain, and a look at the future directions in this exciting research field.

2 Recent Progress and Research Questions

The state-of-the-art research in the fields of biometric recognition, multi-modal and cancelable biometrics, artificial biometrics and social behavioral biometrics is led by a team of researchers at the Biometric technologies laboratory, the University of Calgary, Canada. Social behavioral pattern analysis is the emerging domain in the biometric recognition; the idea behind it is to extract behavioral clues from the everyday human interactions. Activity-related biometric authentication provides an unobtrusive and natural alternative for physiological biometric that can exploit everyday life activities involving interaction with objects or people for extracting biometric signature. In 2015, (Drosou et al. 2015) introduced a new activity biometric based on the motion patterns of prehension movement. In the same year, (Bazazian and Gavrilova 2015) utilized behavioral and social contextual metadata to increase the recognition performance of gait recognition based on multimodal fusion. Their proposed method exploited the daily routine activities of users to extract important behavioral patterns and contextual information using a context extractor and matcher. In recent years, the mass growth of online social networks has introduced a completely new platform of analyzing human behavior. Recent studies showed that behavioral footprints exist in online interactions of users via online social media (Sultana et al. 2014a, Sultana et al. 2014b, Sultana et al. 2016) Another recent research showed that editing behavior of users in collaborative environment such as Wikipedia can help to predict the identity of authors (Paul et al. 2015). In these works, analysis of social data over a period of time explores underlying behavioral pattern and demonstrated encouraging performance in user identification. Authors identified online social behavioral interactions as the potential candidates of behavioral biometrics. The applications of the proposed social behavioral biometrics features are as diverse as person authentication, access control, anomaly detection, customer profiling, behavior analysis, situation awareness, risk analysis, friend recommendation systems, and so on.

Social interactions were traditionally investigated by social scientists, psychologists, bankers, advertisers, recruiters and therapists. Biometric technologies Laboratory at the University of Calgary pioneered the research in the Social Behavioural Biometrics, where online network users' social traits are studied with the goal of understanding discriminative traits, which can be subsequently used for user recognition. Research presented in 2017 papers appeared in IEEE Transactions on Human Computer Interactions and IEEE Transactions on System, Men and Cybernetics (Sultana et al. 2017a, Sultana et al. 2017b), established Social Behaviour as one of the biometric traits suitable for accurate user authentication, and establish some properties of those biometrics, such as discriminability, universality and permanence. The main research questions that were answered are:

(1) *Can a user recognition be accomplished from user social interactions and online social activities?*

(2) *What properties the social biometric features possess (i.e. uniqueness, stability, discriminability)?*
(3) *Will frequency of data collection affect recognition behavior of biometric system based on Social Biometric features?*
(4) *Is it feasible to build a multi-modal system based on a combination of social and traditional (physiological and behavioral) features.*

This pioneering work represents the first comprehensive study of social interactions as a behavioral biometric, leading the way towards intelligent situation aware systems.

3 Social Behavioural Biometrics

It has been previously established by the Biometric Technologies laboratory researchers that social network analysis can provide an additional clue on how social behaviour can be used for user identification in security centred systems (Sultana et al. 2014a, Sultana et al. 2015). The implications of this work are significant. It is the first step towards a new generation of biometric systems that are capable of understanding and interpreting social actions and behaviours, and utilizing them for security purposes. Combined with powerful cognitive architectures, the social behavioural based systems tend to mimic human brain processes related to person identification. It is well known that emotional responses, adaptive behaviour, complex decision making, contextual information processing and emotional associations play a significant role in how human recognize each other (Haxby et al. 2002). Thus, the more knowledge about a person can be extracted, the better recognition results might become. Thus, researchers envision the next generation biometric systems as intelligent machines capable of utilizing all aspects of information (physiological, behavioural, and social) in order to make a confident human-like decision in unfavourable conditions, where the traditional biometrics would not perform well (Gavrilova et al. 2016). In the recently published book chapter, we postulate that 'the next generation biometric systems should be equipped with the mechanisms of extracting social features from the everyday social interactions of individuals, adaptively expanding behavioural patterns as well as learning new knowledge by analysing those features over time. Thus, those behavioural and social patterns will be utilized to authenticate individuals with higher confidence even in the absence of other traditional biometric traits' (Gavrilova et al. 2016).

In addition to traditional means of human authentication, based on well-known biometrics such as face, fingerprint, iris, ear, voice and gait, the information obtained from the social interaction can enhance performance capabilities of traditional decision making systems. Our research showed that it is possible to fuse such social information with existing physiological or behavioral biometrics as part of a multimodal system to make a confident decision on the person's identity. Figure 1 presents a generalized framework of the developed social biometric system. Figure 2 provides classification of possible on-line interactions. The system architecture demonstrates that auxiliary features (e.g. social behavioral features, contextual information, spatio-temporal traits) and soft biometrics (e.g. aesthetic preference, age, gender, affiliation, hobbies etc.) can be extracted from routine social activities of a person observed in online or off-line social environments (e.g. meeting room, family gathering, office, classroom, chat room, facebook, twitter, etc.). During an enrollment phase, biometric features are extracted from physiological and behavioral traits as well as from social data in a given social space. All features are stored in the training database as biometric profiles of enrolled individuals. During an authentication phase, physiological, behavioral, and social features can be used individually or in a combination with others. At the identification or verification stage, matching module will compared stored profiles with user being tested by the system, and the decision will be made based on the closeness of the match between user testing and training profiles. The main advantage of the proposed fusion of social data and soft biometrics is that a reliable authentication decision can be obtained from the biometric systems regardless of the distortion or missing features of the physiological or behavioral biometrics (Sultana et al. 2017a, Sultana et al. 2017b).

Knowledge about individuals' social behaviour can also be obtained by mining their social data in a particular social space (Sultana et al. 2014a, Sultana et al. 2015). For instance, a person's close friend list can be obtained by keeping a record of his accompanying persons over time. In this way, analysing social data may reveal valuable information about a person including personal choice, preference, social acquaintances, contextual and spatio-temporal information. This information can be directly exploited as soft biometrics during biometric authentication. Alternately, unique social behavioural patterns can be exploited as a modality of biometric trait and fused at feature, match score, rank, or decision levels. One of the intriguing phenomena is that social behavioural biometrics can be extracted by observing the known behavioural biometrics (e.g. expression, interactions, gestures, voice, activities etc.) of individuals in a specific social setting over a period. For instance, an idiosyncratic way of starting a speech of a person can be revealed by analyzing voice data acquired from regular meetings, which can act as social behavioral biometric during authentication (Sultana et al. 2014a).

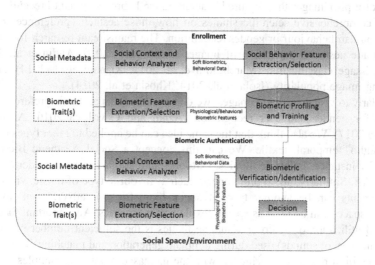

Fig. 1. A generalized flow diagram of the enrollment and authentication system, using fusion of social, contextual, behavioral and physiological data (Gavrilova et al. 2016).

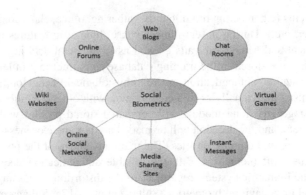

Fig. 2. Some on-line application domains of social biometrics (Gavrilova et al. 2016).

4   Social Aesthetic Biometrics

On-line interactions can be expressed as tweets, posts, opinions, wiki-entries, games, avatar behaviors, and other ways users express themselves over social networks. Even interaction with close family members can now take place over a variety of online social networks (Facebook, Twitter, Pinterest, Flickr, YouTube etc.). Users express their opinions, relationship status, preferences, political views, and even aesthetic preferences through text, images and videos. In one of the recent studies, Flickr dataset images were mapped to user preferences and subsequently used to analytically evaluate an impact that artistic preferences can have on a human's behaviour (Lovato et al. 2014, Segalin et al. 2014). In those works, a set of heterogeneous image features was used to build the visual preference model of a person that can distinguish that person from others. Another image based online social network is Pinterest, where a person can mark (or pin) images that capture his attention while browsing. Until recently, there were no comprehensive scientific studies on how those aesthetic preferences can be used for human behaviour or gender recognition. The mainstream research focused on an automatic aesthetic evaluation of images (Jiang et al. 2010, Aydin et al. 2015), aesthetic image classification (Marchesotti et al. 2011, Xiaohui et al. 2014), and on estimating image popularity (Isola et al. 2014, Khosla et al. 2014).

Similarly to visual aesthetic images, we demonstrated that aesthetic preferences can be used for gender and user recognition (Azam and Gavrilova 2016, Azam and Gavrilova 2017). We also think that the same idea can be applied to other types of data: visual, audio, temporal, textile. We call this concept a Social Aesthetic Biometrics (SAB). For instance, favourite movies, cartoons, animations can be considered a new type of SAB. Similarly, audio preferences, such as favourite type of music, video clips or instruments can be another type of social biometric. Moreover, even favourite fabrics or spaces can be used as spatial textile soft biometrics. An important factor for successful utilization of audio or visual aesthetics is the sufficient number of samples (such as images, or sounds) used during template generation and matching. Typically, a high recognition rate can be achieved with the increased number of samples.

Person's aesthetic preference is a recent addition to the social biometric traits. The intuition is that a person can be characterized in a distinct way using his personal taste, preferences, and likes. However, this social biometric trait still needs to be investigated thoroughly to consider its uniqueness, stability over time and differentiating features.

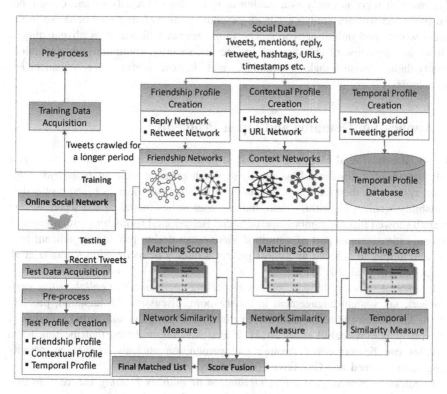

Fig. 3. Social biometric system architecture (Sultana et al. 2017a).

5 Multi-modal Fusion of Traditional and Social Biometrics

In addition to the new research directions outlined above, another emerging research domain is design and development of a multi-modal biometric system, which fuses traditional and novel biometric modalities. Some of the recent works in this domain considered various multi-modal system architectures, including rank and match level fusion, Markov chain and neural-network based models, fuzzy and cognitive architectures (Wang et al. 2016, Tian et al. 2011). This research also focused on how to identify the most appropriate machine learning algorithm for improved classification, and how to design an adaptive biometric system that will perform well regardless of the data quality (Gavrilova and Monwar 2013). In 2017, researchers from the BT Lab proposed to fuse the social behavioral information obtained from the online social networks with physiological biometrics (Sultana et al. 2017a, Sultana et al. 2017b).

This study demonstrated that the social interactions of individuals via online social media possess biometric distinctiveness, thus making them suitable to be treated as behavioral modality to enhance intelligent decision making and accuracy of a multi-modal biometric system. An architecture of a system module responsible for extracting biometric features from Twitter social data, shown in Fig. 3. This cutting edge research serve not only as a trailblazer in intelligent security system design, but also paves the way for studying human psychology as well as social behavior in the virtual worlds and online networks. The future research direction worth pursuing is real-world integration of this research in forensic, security, continuous authentication, identity-theft, decision-making training, and human performance enhancement technologies.

6 Application Domains and Open Problems

The social behavioural biometrics described in this article can find applications in a wide spectrum of domains. First of all, they can enhance existing *biometric multi-modal systems*, as their current performance still varies significantly based on the data availability, quality, algorithms used, training approaches foretaken and so on. Recent research showed that the combination of Social Behavioural Biometrics with traditional biometric identifiers as part of a multi-modal system design provides significant benefits and allows to achieve an almost perfect accuracy of recognition (Sultana et al. 2017a, Sultana et al. 2017b).

In a social sciences domain, studies evaluating *engagement in collaborative environments*, **i.e.** student engagement in a classroom, discussion participation, problem solving facilitation and so on can be evaluated by analysing the non-verbal activities of the participants (Whitehill et al. 2014). It also was demonstrated that meeting room activities can be monitored through gait recognition analysis as well as activity recognition (Ahmed and Gavrilova 2015, Ahmed et al. 2015).

Needless to mention, *athlete rehabilitation or military training* can rely on biometric emotion analysis. For instance, the degree of pain, the state of depression or a presence of others psychological impediments as well as an emotional state of a person can be understood from facial expressions or body language (Vinciarelli et al. 2012). Automatic detection offline or in real time of various behavioural patterns can be helpful in the treatment of psychological disorders as well as in medicine in general.

In addition to military training and medical applications, an early detection of certain physiological patterns such as anxiety or depression can assist with *security and risk assessment*. Such situation awareness systems can be used at border control or at the entrance to secure locations or events through the screening or in surveillance areas (Poursaberi et al. 2013).

In *marketing*, audience understanding and user profiling has been one of the key factors in the ad campaigns. With availability of low cost advertisement options, such as Facebook pages, online news sections and YouTube channels, Recent studies demonstrated that emotional responses towards an advertisement can accurately predict the marketing success of the new product (McDuff et al. 2015). A similar tactics are used in banking and other consumer oriented domains. Blogging activities on facebook or a twitter can provide significant information about user preferences, likes, and intentions (Sultana et al. 2014, Sultana et al. 2015, Paul et al. 2015). In addition, aesthetic preferences of individuals can also be analysed to positively impact a targeted advertisement, or a political campaign, thus giving rise to Social Aesthetic Biometrics (Azam and Gavrilova 2015, Azam and Gavrilova 2017).

Even the *virtual world* interactions can be useful to understand human behaviour better. An avatar or a virtual agents is a projection of a person's personality on a virtual world. Studies in the Artimetrics, aka Artificial Biometrics, showed that some users channel their real world personal and exhibit social behavioural traits in the virtual environments (Yampolskiy and Gavrilova 2012, Gavrilova and Yampolskiy 2011). Virtual agents can also exhibit various emotions through their facial expressions, body position or an attitude during a virtual world interactions (Vinciarelli et al. 2012). Social behavioural traits, thus, can be extracted from user behaviour in the virtual worlds, in addition to off-line and on-line social networks. This opens up almost unlimited possibilities to utilize virtual worlds for real-life training and decision-making, and to study group dynamics or extreme situation responses in the simulated scenarios.

7 Conclusions

This Editor-in-Chief position paper provides an overview of the current state-of-the-art in the biometric security and discusses its links to online user behaviour in virtual worlds. It describes the new research sub-area: Social Biometrics, and discusses how it physiological, behavioural, and social characteristics of humans and avatars can be analysed and modelled. Social Aesthetic Biometrics as well as Artificial Biometrics, or ArtiMetrics, are also mentioned as some of the emerging research directions. A discussion on how biometric traits can be extrapolated from social, contextual, temporal, aesthetic, virtual world behavioural data of individuals is also presented. The presented position paper also emphasizes the importance of further collaborative research in the domains of virtual worlds and online security.

Acknowledgments. We would like to acknowledge NSERC Discovery Grant RT731064, as well as MITACS agency for partial support of this research.

References

Ahmed, F., Gavrilova, M.: Biometric-based user authentication and activity level detection in a collaborative environment. In: Matei, S.A., Russell, M.G., Bertino, E. (eds.) Transparency in Social Media. CSS, pp. 165–180. Springer, Cham (2015). doi:10.1007/978-3-319-18552-1_9

Ahmed, F., Paul, P., Gavrilova, M.: Dtw-based kernel and rank level fusion for 3d gait recognition using Kinect. Vis. Comput. **31**(6–8), 915–924 (2015)

Aydin, T., Smolic, A., Gross, M.: Automated aesthetic analysis of photographic images. IEEE Trans. Vis. Comput. Graph. **21**(1), 31–42 (2015)

Azam, S., Gavrilova, M.: Person identification using discriminative visual aesthetic. In: Mouhoub, M., Langlais, P. (eds.) AI 2017. LNCS, vol. 10233, pp. 15–26. Springer, Cham (2017). doi:10.1007/978-3-319-57351-9_2

Azam, S., Gavrilova, M.: Gender prediction using individual perceptual image aesthetics. J. Winter Sch. Comput. Graph. (WSCG) 24(02), 53–62 (2016)

Barakova, E., Gorbunov, R., Rauterberg, M.: Automatic interpretation of affective facial expressions in the context of interpersonal interaction. IEEE Trans. Hum. Mach. Syst. 45(4), 409–418 (2015)

Bazazian, S., Gavrilova, M.: A hybrid method for context-based gait recognition based on behavioral and social traits. In: Gavrilova, M.L., Tan, C.K., Saeed, K., Chaki, N., Shaikh, S. H. (eds.) Transactions on Computational Science XXV. LNCS, vol. 9030, pp. 115–134. Springer, Heidelberg (2015). doi:10.1007/978-3-662-47074-9_7

Chew, S., Lucey, P., Lucey, S., Saragih, J., Cohn, J., Matthews, I., Sridharan, S.: In the pursuit of effective affective computing: the relationship between features and registration. IEEE Trans. Syst. Man Cybern. B, 42(4), pp. 1006–1016 (2012)

Drosou, A., Ioannidisa, D., Tzovarasa, D., Moustakasb, K., Petroua, M.: Activity related authentication using prehension biometrics. Pattern Recogn. 48(5), 1743–1759 (2015)

Gavrilova, M.L., Ahmed, F., Azam, S., Paul, P.P., Rahman, W., Sultana, M., Zohra, F.T.: Emerging trends in security system design using the concept of social behavioural biometrics. In: Alsmadi, I.M., Karabatis, G., AlEroud, A. (eds.) Information Fusion for Cyber-Security Analytics. SCI, vol. 691, pp. 229–251. Springer, Cham (2017). doi:10.1007/978-3-319-44257-0_10

Gavrilova, M., Monwar, M.: Multimodal biometrics and intelligent image processing for security systems, IGI book (2013)

Gavrilova, M.L., Yampolskiy, R.: Applying biometric principles to avatar recognition. In: Gavrilova, M.L., Tan, C.J.K., Sourin, A., Sourina, O. (eds.) Transactions on Computational Science XII. LNCS, vol. 6670, pp. 140–158. Springer, Heidelberg (2011). doi:10.1007/978-3-642-22336-5_8

Gavrilova, M.: Emerging directions in biometric security research, report prepared for cognition and computation group for the DRDC Workshop on HSP 2017 (submitted) (2017)

Haxby, J., Hoffman, E., Gobbini, I.: Human neural systems for face recognition and social communication. Biol. Psychiatry 51(1), 59–67 (2002)

Isola, P., Xiao, J., Parikh, D., Torralba, A., Oliva, A.: What makes a photograph memorable? IEEE Trans. Pattern Anal. Mach. Intell. 36(7), 1469–1482 (2014)

Jain, A.K., Ross, A., Prabhakar, S.: An introduction to biometric recognition. IEEE Trans. Circ. Syst Video Technol. 14(1), 420 (2004)

Jiang, W., Loui, A., Cerosaletti, C.: Automatic aesthetic value assessment in photographic images. In: 2010 IEEE International Conference on Multimedia and Expo (ICME), pp. 920-925 (2010)

Khosla, A., Sarma, A.D., Hamid, R.: What makes an image popular?. In: 23rd International Conference on World wide web (WWW 2014), pp. 867-876 (2014)

Li, Y., Wang, S., Zhao, Y., Ji, Q.: Simultaneous facial feature tracking and facial expression recognition. IEEE Trans. Image Proces. 22(7), 2559–2573 (2013)

Littlewort, G., Whitehill, J., Wu, T., Fasel, I., Frank, M., Movellan, J., Bartlett, M.: The computer expression recognition toolbox (CERT). In: International Conference on Automatic Face Gesture Recognition, pp. 298–305 (2011)

Lovato, P., Bicego, M., Segalin, C., Perina, A., Sebe, N., Cristani, M.: Faved! biometrics: tell me which image you like and I'll tell you who you are. IEEE Trans IFS 9(3), 364–374 (2014)

Marchesotti, L., Perronnin, F., Larlus, D., Csurka, G.: Assessing the aesthetic quality of photographs using generic image descriptors. In: IEEE International Conference Computer Vision (ICCV), pp. 1784-1791 (2011)

McDuff, D., Kaliouby, R., Cohn, J.F., Picard, R.W.: Predicting ad liking and purchase intent: large-scale analysis of facial responses to Ads. IEEE Trans Affect. Comp. 6(3), 223–235 (2015)

Paul, P.P., Gavrilova, M.L., Alhajj, R.: Decision fusion for multimodal biometrics using social network analysis systems. IEEE Trans. Syst. Man Cybern. Syst. 44(11), 522–1533 (2014)

Paul, P.P., Sultana, M., Matei, S.A., Gavrilova, M.L.: Editing behavior to recognize authors of crowdsourced content. In: IEEE International Conference on SMC, pp. 1676-1681 (2015)

Poursaberi, A., Vana, J., Mráček, S., Dvora, R., Yanushkevich, S.N., Drahansky, M., Shmerko, V.P., Gavrilova, M.L.: Facial biometrics for situational awareness systems. IET Biometrics 2 (2), 35–47 (2013)

Ross, A., Nandakumar, K., Jain, A.K.: Handbook of Multibiometrics. Springer, Berlin (2006). doi:10.1007/0-387-33123-9

Segalin, C., Perina, A., Cristani, M.: Personal aesthetics for soft biometrics: a generative multi-resolution approach. In: 16th International Conference on Multimodal Interaction (ICMI 2014), pp. 180-187 (2014)

Sultana, M., Paul, P.P., Gavrilova, M.: Mining social behavioral biometrics in twitter. In: International Conference on Cyberworlds, pp. 293-299 (2014b)

Sultana, M, Paul, P.P., Gavrilova, M.: A concept of social behavioral biometrics: motivation, current developments, and future trends. In: International Conference on Cyberworlds, pp. 271-278 (2014a)

Sultana, M., Paul, P.P., Gavrilova, M.: Identifying users from online interactions in twitter. In: Gavrilova, M.L., Tan, C.J.K., Iglesias, A., Shinya, M., Galvez, A., Sourin, A. (eds.) Transactions on Computational Science XXVI. LNCS, vol. 9550, pp. 111–124. Springer, Heidelberg (2016). doi:10.1007/978-3-662-49247-5_7

Sultana, M., Paul, P.P., Gavrilova, M.: Person recognition from social behavior in computer mediated social contex. In: IEEE Transactions Human Machine Systems, Early Access, Print and Online (http://ieeexplore.ieee.org/document/789160) March 2017b

Sultana, M., Paul, P.P., Gavrilova, M.: Social behavioral information fusion in multimodal biometrics. In: IEEE Transactions SMC: Systems, Early Access Print ISSN: 2168-2216, Online ISSN: 2168-2232, April 2017a

Sultana, M., Paul, P.P., Gavrilova, M.: Social behavioral biometrics: an emerging trend. Int J. Pattern Recogn. Artif. Intell. 29(8), 1556013-1-20 (2015)

Tian, Y., Wang, Y., Gavrilova, M., Ruhe, G.: A formal knowledge representation system (FKRS) for the intelligent knowledge base of a cognitive learning engine. Int. J. Softw. Sci. Comput. Intell. 3, 1–17 (2011)

Vinciarelli, A., Pantic, M., Heylen, D., Pelachaud, C., Poggi, I., Errico, F.D., Schroeder, M.: Bridging the gap between social animal and unsocial machine: a survey of social signal processing. IEEE Trans. Affect. Comput. 3(1), 69–87 (2012)

Wang, Y., Widrow, B., Zadeh, L.A., Howard, N., Wood, S.V., Bhavsar, C., Budin, G., Chan, C., Fiorini, R.A., Gavrilova, M.L., Shell, D.F.: Cognitive intelligence: deep learning, thinking, and reasoning by brain-inspired systems. IJCINI 10(4), 1–20 (2016)

Whitehill, J., Serpell, Z., Lin, Y.C., Foster, A., Movellan, J.R.: The faces of engagement: automatic recognition of student engagement from facial expressions. IEEE Trans. Affect. Comput. 5(1), 86–98 (2014)

Xiaohui, W., Jia, J., Yin, J., Cai, L.: Interpretable aesthetic features for affective image classification. In: 20th IEEE International Conference on Image Processing (ICIP), pp. 3230-3234 (2014)

Yampolskiy, R., Gavrilova, M.: Artimetrics: biometrics for artificial entities. IEEE Robot. Autom. Mag. 19(4), 48–58 (2012)

KINECT Face Recognition Using Occluded Area Localization Method

Fatema Tuz Zohra[✉] and Marina Gavrilova

Department of Computer Science, Faculty of Science, University of Calgary,
2500 University Drive N.W., Calgary, AB T2N 1N4, Canada
fatematuz.zohra@ucalgary.ca, marina@cpsc.ucalgary.ca

Abstract. Automated face recognition is commonly used for security reinforcement and identity verification purposes. While significant advancement has been made in this domain, modern surveillance techniques are still dependent on variations in pose, orientation of the facial images, difference in the illumination, occlusion, etc. Therefore, face recognition or identification in uncontrolled situations has become an important research topic. In this paper, we propose a new face recognition technique that takes into account partial occlusion, while still accurately identifying the user. The occluded facial areas are detected from the Kinect depth images by extracting features using Uniform Local Binary Pattern (LBP). For localizing occluded regions from the Kinect depth images, a threshold based approach is used to identify the areas close to the camera. The recognition system will discard the occluded regions of the facial images and match only the non-occluded facial part with the gallery of images to find the best possible match. The performance of the recognition system has been evaluated on EUROKOM Kinect face database containing different types of occluded and non-occluded faces with neutral expressions. Experimental results show that the proposed method improves the recognition rate by 4.8% and 5.7% for occlusion by hand and occlusion by paper, respectively.

Keywords: Kinect sensor · Depth images · Binary classifier · KNN classifier · Occlusion detection · Face recognition using depth information

1 Introduction

Automatic face recognition has established itself as a key research area in computer vision and pattern recognition over the past few decades. Face biometric based identification is one of the most popular and highly accepted biometric traits due to its non-invasive nature of the acquisition process. Over the years, face biometric has been extensively investigated to improve the recognition performance. However, despite many years of research, face biometric recognition is still an active domain due to the challenges in identifying the faces in unconstrained environments. These include different illumination, expression and pose variance, deformation due to aging, and different types of occlusions [4,11,15,19].

© Springer-Verlag GmbH Germany 2017
M.L. Gavrilova et al. (Eds.): Trans. on Comput. Sci. XXX, LNCS 10560, pp. 12–28, 2017.
https://doi.org/10.1007/978-3-662-56006-8_2

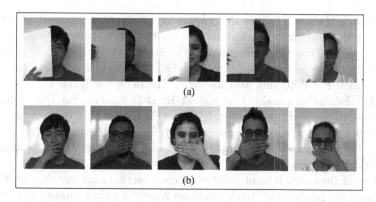

Fig. 1. Example of occluded RGB facial images from EURECOM Kinect Face dataset [20]. (a) occlusion by paper, and (b) occlusion by hand. (Color figure online)

Handling occlusions during face automation of security systems is a challenging task. Due to occlusions, different facial parts are not visible and also inaccessible during face recognition, which make it difficult to effectively recognize faces in the presence of occlusion. Sometimes it is not possible to extract distinctive facial information from the face in the presence of occlusion, which may result in false identification of the person. It should be treated carefully as it can undermine the correct performance of a surveillance system. Some recent research shows that, face recognition systems that use 3D or 2.5D (depth) information have more efficient recognition than the 2D based face recognition systems [2,3,7,13,20,23]. This is due to the fact that illumination invariant 3D information, such as depth information and a shape of a face can be incorporated with the 2D information to improve the accuracy of the recognition. However, these recognition methods also generate inferior results for facial expression and occlusion variations. Therefore, it is necessary to build a system that can effectively recognize faces in the presence of occlusion. To address this challenge, we propose a new face recognition system that will take into account the occluded area of the faces while identifying the user.

Recently, RGB-D cameras such as Kinect sensor have received a vast amount of attention from diverse research communities [12,14,16,26,27] as it is a low cost device which can effectively extract the depth mapping from the object in front of the camera. Kinect sensor can capture 2D and 3D data simultaneously with a promising acquisition time. Therefore, researchers investigated the Kinect Face datasets [20] for the purpose of face recognition, face salient points localization, occlusion detection, 3D modeling of the faces and emotion recognition. There is very limited research that concentrates on face recognition in the presence of occlusion using the depth information. Therefore, in this paper, we propose a novel face recognition system that will consider the occluded area localized from Kinect depth images while identifying the user from the gallery facial images. If the probe image contains occluded area, then the face recognition system will match only the non-occluded facial parts with the gallery images to find the best possible match. This will reduce the number of misclassification, and as a result, will improve the recognition performance of the biometric system. We extract the local features from the facial images using Local Binary Pattern (LBP) analysis and feed those features to the k-nearest neighbor (KNN) classifier to identify the occluded faces. For detecting and localizing the occluded facial areas we used the depth information provided by Kinect RGB-D camera. For the evaluation of the proposed method, we consider EURECOM Kinect Face dataset [20]. This journal paper is an extended version of the research presented in Cyberworlds 2016 [34]. Figure 1 shows an example of occluded RGB facial images from the EURECOM Kinect Face dataset.

The rest of the paper is structured as follows. Section 2 presents a comprehensive study of the previous research works on Kinect database and face occlusion detection approaches based on depth information. In Sect. 3 detailed description of the proposed method for face recognition using occluded area localized from Kinect depth images is presented. The experimental setup and results are shown in Sect. 4. Finally, Sect. 5 concludes the discussion with some future directions.

2   Literature Review

Occlusion detection has been extensively studied in the literature. Many approaches have been proposed to detect 2D faces under occlusions. Some of the very recent approaches [10, 18, 19, 33] can accurately detect the occlusion in 2D facial images. An effective method for occlusion detection based on the structured sparse representation is used to estimate the error introduced by occlusion in [18]. The authors used a morphological graph model and localized similarity measure to detect the error. The proposed method can handle high level of occlusion. In [10], the authors proposed an approach to detect half occluded faces in an unconstrained crowd scene. It used a machine learning approach and trained the classifier with left and right half occluded faces. The authors proposed a free rectangular feature to modify the Viola-Jones algorithm for detecting the occluded faces. They also applied skin color models to improve the correctness of the system. The proposed method is evaluated on FDDB dataset. The first occlusion detection method based on multi-task convolution neural network (CNN) was proposed in [33]. The authors pre-trained the CNN model with non-occluded facial images of different orientations. After that, they fine-tuned all the convolution filter using the deep FO datasets and determined the occluded facial parts. The proposed method shows accuracy of 100% and 97.24% while evaluating on the AR face dataset and FO dataset respectively.

Recently, researchers have focused on face recognition based on 2.5D and 3D facial images [2, 3, 7, 13, 20, 23]. However, there is very limited research on occlusion detection and localization based on depth images. In [5], the authors proposed an automated approach that can detect, normalize and recognize faces in the presence of extraneous objects from depth images. They built a non-occluded face model using eigenfaces approach and compared every part of the face with this model. Any part that did not match with the model was identified as the occluded facial part. They tested their proposed approach on UND database processed with an artificial occlusion generator. Their method could detect 83.8% of the occluded faces. The main deficiency of this approach is that it used artificially generated occlusions which may not reflect the real environment. The authors of [1] proposed an occlusion detection method for unconstrained three-dimensional (3D) facial identification. They used a nose-based registration of the facial image to align the input face with a generic face model. The occluded areas are detected by computing the absolute difference between the input face and the generic face model. For evaluation, they considered Bosphorus 3D face database resulting in an accuracy of 94.23%. For the nose-based registration to work, the nose area should be visible. Otherwise, the proposed method will fail. In [28], the authors proposed a similar approach as [5] for occlusion detection based on 3D face restoration. They used Gappy Principal Component Analysis (GPCA) for the restoration process. Two subsequent steps- initial 3D occlusion detection and refined 3D occlusion calculation - are used to determine the location of the occlusion. The proposed method generates an average recognition accuracy of 93.03% on UMB-DB database. In the recent paper on occlusion detection and localization [9], the authors proposed a threshold and block based approach using depth images. The depth images are processed to detect the outward sections of the face using Energy Range Face Images to identify the occluded region. The accuracy of the threshold based technique is 91.79% and the accuracy of the block based approach is 99.71% on Bosphorus database. In this method, facial image with two outward regions is identified as the occluded facial image, where one of the outward regions is nose and another one is the occluded area. However, this method will not work for the input images where the nose area is occluded. In [8], the authors proposed an occlusion detection approach that projects the facial parts into two local subspaces: PCA and two-dimensional LDA. The authors of [8] used Viola Jones algorithm to separate every facial parts and in the classification stage individually recognized each part. They used a threshold value to classify occluded and non-occluded facial parts. The proposed method was evaluated on three different databases. The accuracy of occlusion detection is 62.97% (for 2DPCA). This is the only work that considered the Kinect face dataset [20] for occlusion detection. However, they used the 2D facial images captured using Kinect sensor.

All these papers focus on occlusion detection based on 2.5D and 3D face information acquired using 3D scanners, which requires relatively high data acquisition time. However, for an effective face automation and security surveillance the data acquisition time should be lower. Therefore, in this paper, we focus on facial data captured using Kinect sensor due to its low data acquisition time. We use an occlusion detection method based on Kinect depth information. The occluded regions are located in the facial images based on the depth information. The proposed face recognition technique will utilize this depth information while identifying faces under partial occlusions. The occluded facial parts will be ignored in the recognition technique for improving the performance.

3   Methodology

Human visual system has the perception of depth. But depth information is absent in the 2D imaging system. Existing research that utilized 2.5D or 3D images for face recognition or occlusion detection uses relatively slow 3D scanners [17,24]. Kinect sensor has the RGB camera to capture RGB images, as well as an infrared (IR) laser emitter and an IR camera to act as a depth sensor [20]. Thus, Kinect sensor can capture the 2D and 3D data simultaneously with a promising acquisition time. It can build an effective depth map with varying intensity values based on the distance from the camera. The high intensity value means the object is closer to the camera and low intensity depicts the object is further from the camera. In this paper, we proposed a face recognition method that will consider the depth information acquired using the Kinect RGB-D camera for identifying faces in the presence of occlusion. The proposed method has four steps, namely: (i) preprocessing, (ii) occlusion detection, (iii) occlusion localization and (iv) face recognition under occlusion. We use LBP operators to analyze the local patterns and SVM as a binary classifier to determine whether it is a front face or an occluded face. After that, occlusions are localized in those detected occluded facial images. The face recognition system considers only the non-occluded area while identifying the user from the occluded facial images.

3.1   Preprocessing

The Kinect face database contains manually annotated facial salient points, such as left eye center, right eye center, nose-tip, left mouth corner, right mouth corner and chin. The first step in preprocessing is to crop the facial images using those six anchor points on a face. These facial points can also be extracted using Viola-Jones algorithm [32]. Figure 2(a) and (b) show example of cropped occluded face RGB and depth images, respectively.

The next step is to normalize the depth values in the cropped facial image. For that, we consider only the average $\pm$ maximum gray values (consider other values as zero), and scale it into the range 0 to 1. Figure 2(c) shows an example of normalized depth images. In a depth image, intensity values indicate estimated distances from the camera [25]. The facial images are normalized to emphasize the difference in depth for different facial parts. Figure 3(a) shows an example of the front face image before normalization and Fig. 3(b) depicts an example of front face image after normalization. Here, x and y axis represent the size of the image, and z axis represents the depth values. From the figure we can see that the differences in depth for different facial parts is more visible in the normalized version of facial images. Also, we can see that intensity values indicate estimated distances from the camera. In Fig. 3(b) red pixels represent the object closer to the camera. If there is any occlusion presents in the facial image, then it will have lower distance from the camera which can be estimated from the pixel values. Figure 4(a) and (b) show examples of normalized depth images of a face occluded by hand and paper respectively. Here, x and y axis represent the size of the image, and z axis represents the depth values. The marked area

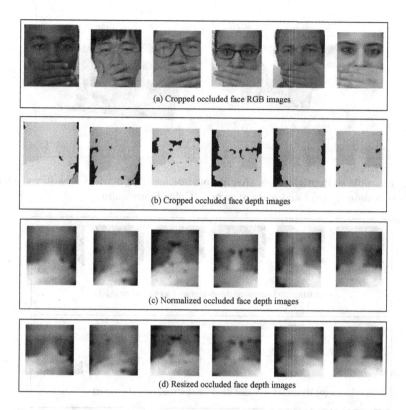

Fig. 2. Example of occluded (occlusion by hand) facial images from EURECOM Kinect Face dataset [20]. (a) cropped RGB images, (b) cropped depth images, (c) normalized depth images, and (d) resized depth images. (Color figure online)

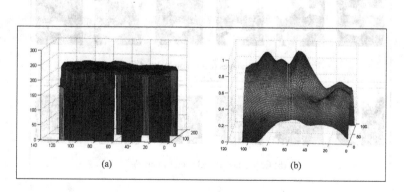

Fig. 3. Example of front face image plotted using Matlab *surface plot* operation (a) before normalization, and (b) after normalization. (Color figure online)

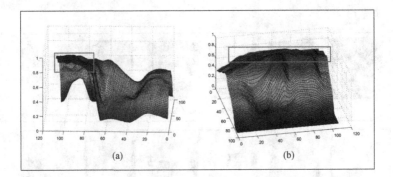

Fig. 4. Example of depth images after preprocessing. The marked area in red pixels depicts occlusion by (a) hand and (b) paper. (Color figure online)

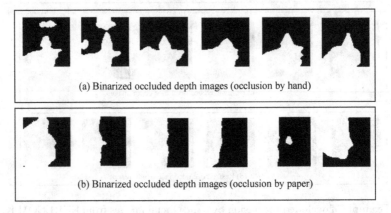

(a) Binarized occluded depth images (occlusion by hand)

(b) Binarized occluded depth images (occlusion by paper)

Fig. 5. Example of occluded facial images after thresholding and noise removal, (a) occluded by hand, and (b) occluded by paper.

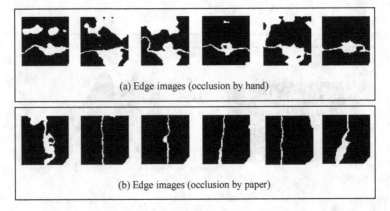

(a) Edge images (occlusion by hand)

(b) Edge images (occlusion by paper)

Fig. 6. Example of edge images computed from the absolute difference of reference and occluded depth images, (a) occluded by hand, and (b) occluded by paper.

in Fig. 4(a) and (b) represents the position of hand and paper in front of face. From the figure we can see that the occluded regions have different pixel values than the other facial parts and are identifiable from the facial image. The last step in preprocessing is to down-sample the facial image in a 64×64 region using bicubic interpolation. Figure 2(d) shows an example of resized depth images.

3.2   Occlusion Detection

After preprocessing of the facial images, features are extracted from the normalized and resized images using uniform local binary patterns (LBP) [21,22]. LBP is a powerful operator to analyze the local pattern. It generates a binary number by thresholding the neighbors of each pixel for labeling the pixels in the image. LBP is used extensively in local pattern analysis for its discriminating power and computational simplicity. In [20], the authors showed that for analyzing depth images, LBP works better than other feature extraction operators, such as Principle Component Analysis (PCA), Scale-invariant feature transform (SIFT) and Local Gabor binary pattern (LGBP). Thus, for our proposed method we use uniform Local Binary Patterns for feature extraction. The notation for uniform LBP is $LBP_{(P,R)}^{u2}$ where P is the number of neighbors on a circle of radius R [21,22]. The occurrences of the uniform pattern codes are extracted from the image and placed into a histogram. For our proposed method, we extract the feature histogram for different neighborhood and radius, and examine which LBP operator performs better. The investigation shows that among $LBP_{(8,1)}^{u2}$, $LBP_{(8,2)}^{u2}$ and $LBP_{(16,2)}^{u2}$ operators, $LBP_{(8,2)}^{u2}$ results in better classification accuracy for detecting front and occluded faces. Therefore, to better capture the difference between the front face and occluded face from depth images, we derive a facial representation using $LBP_{(8,2)}^{u2}$ operator which yields a feature vector of length 59.

After computing the feature histogram from the facial images using $LBP_{(8,2)}^{u2}$ operator, we use a binary classifier, support vector machine (SVM) [6] to determine whether the input image corresponds to a frontal view of the face or it contains some kind of occlusions. The classifier is first trained using a set of positive (front faces) and negative (occluded faces) samples for the classification task. In the training phase, the front face images are labeled as binary 1 and occluded facial images (occluded by hand and paper) as binary 0. The computed feature histograms along with the front face-occluded face labeling are fed into the SVM classifier to train the model.

3.3   Occlusion Localization

Investigation on depth images shows that if the face is occluded, then there must be some regions other than the nose area in the face that is closer to the camera. From Fig. 2(d), we can see that the occluded region of the face (occlusion by hand) has higher pixel values in the depth map. The pixel intensity is disproportional to the distance from the camera. Based on this hypothesis, a threshold based approach is proposed to extract high intensity values from the occluded depth images. The facial images are filtered based on empirically set threshold value, T. After that morphological opening operation is applied to the threshold image to remove all the small objects from binary images. In image processing, morphological open operation can be defined as an erosion followed by a dilation operation. It uses a structuring element for both operations. The erosion operation slides the structuring element over an image to find the local minima, and it creates the output matrix from these minimum values. If the neighborhood or structuring element has a center element then the minima is placed in that place. Similarly, in dilation operation the structuring element is rotated 180°. Then the structuring element is slid over an image to find the local maxima, and to create the output matrix from these maximum values.

Figure 5 shows an example of occluded facial images (occluded by hand and paper) after the thresholding and noise removal step (i.e. morphological opening). In the next step, a component with the maximum energy (i.e. highest pixel intensities) is selected as the potential candidate for the occluded region after connected component analysis on the binary image. Connected-component analysis is an algorithmic application of graph theory. In this analysis, subsets of connected components are uniquely labeled based on a given heuristic. The selected occluded area is then corrected using the reference front face image. In creating the reference image, we have considered the 200 front face images from the database. The absolute difference between the reference image and the occluded facial image will result in an image that has higher pixel values in the area where the difference between the reference and occluded facial image is higher. The resulting images are then binarized to get images with edges at the boundary of the occluded region. In our proposed method, we referred to these images as edge images. Figure 6 shows the example of edge images. In the next step, the selected occluded area after connected component analysis is corrected using the edge images. The edge image contains the boundary of the occluded area. Based on this boundary, the connected component is adjusted to find the accurate occluded area of the facial image. Figure 7 depicts an example of

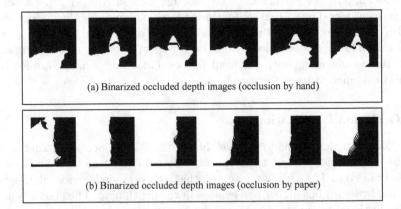

(a) Binarized occluded depth images (occlusion by hand)

(b) Binarized occluded depth images (occlusion by paper)

Fig. 7. Example of occluded facial images after correcting the boundary using edge images, (a) occluded by hand, and (b) occluded by paper.

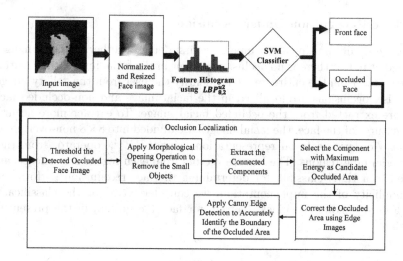

Fig. 8. Steps for occlusion detection and localization from depth images acquired using Kinect.

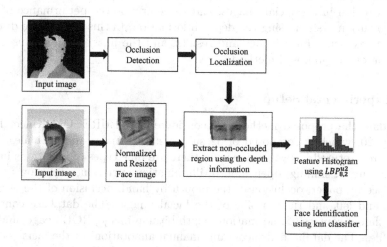

Fig. 9. Generalized block diagram for face recognition in the presence of occlusion.

binarized occluded facial images (occluded by hand and paper) after correcting the occluded region. Finally, we apply canny edge detection to fine tune the boundary of the occluded region. The canny edge detection algorithm can identify a wide range of edges in images. Figure 8 shows the steps for occlusion detection and localization from depth images.

3.4   Face Recognition Under Occlusion

For face recognition using a test image, we first detect whether the facial image is occluded or not. If there is no occlusion present in the facial image, then features are extracted from the entire image to identify the user from the gallery images. Otherwise, occlusions are localized in the facial image and non-occluded facial parts are extracted from the occluded facial image. To extract more accurate local textures of the face, the facial images are divided into 8×8 non-overlapping regions. We derive a facial representation using $LBP_{(8,2)}^{u2}$ operator from those non-overlapping regions. The feature vectors from each region are concatenated and fed to a KNN classifier for determining the face recognition performance. For simplicity of the implementation, we consider KNN for the classification task. Figure 9 shows the block diagram for face recognition in the presence of occlusion.

4   Experimental Results and Discussions

Extensive experimentation has been performed to determine and localize the occluded region in the facial images, and to determine the performance of the face recognition system using the depth information. In this section, we discuss about the experimental settings and results, and the image database used for validation of the proposed method.

4.1   Experimental Setup

To validate the proposed method, we considered the EURECOM Kinect Face Dataset [20] which is composed of 52 subjects: 14 females and 38 males. The images are captured in two sessions and there are nine types of variations in the images: neutral, smiling, open mouth, illumination variation, occlusion of half of the face by paper, occlusion of the mouth by hand, occlusion of the eyes by glasses, and left and right profile of the facial images. The database contains three different sources of information: depth bitmap image, RGB image, and 3D object files. The database also contains manual annotations of the facial salient points. From these sets of images, we considered neutral, illumination variation, occlusion of half of the face and occlusion of the mouth for experimental purpose.

For classifying the images in occluded and non-occluded classes, we used a nonlinear support vector machine (SVM) [6,31] classifier with radial basis kernel to classify front face and occluded face. SVM classifier has a simple geometric interpretation and gives a sparse solution. Moreover, the computational complexity of SVM does not depend on the dimensionality of the input space and it is less prone to over-fitting. Considering all these issues and for the simplicity of implementation, we considered SVM as the classifier for detecting occlusion. The value of sigma for SVM was set empirically. For simplicity and reproduction of the code, other existing parameters were set to their default values according to Matlab function library. For the generalization of the implemented method, 5-fold cross-validation was applied where the training fold contains images of 160 front and 160 occluded faces and the testing fold contains images of 40 front and 40 occluded faces from the database. For the recognition task, K-Nearest Neighbor (KNN) classifier is used with the distance defined as *'cityblock'*. The neutral facial images from session 1 and session 2 were used as gallery images. $LBP^{u2}_{(8,2)}$ operator is used for extracting features from 8×8 non-overlapping regions of the facial images.

4.2 Results and Discussions

For detecting occluded facial images, we consider neutral, light on, occlusion of mouth by hand, and occlusion of face by paper from the database. At first we extracted the individual feature histogram using $LBP^{u2}_{(8,1)}$, $LBP^{u2}_{(8,2)}$ and $LBP^{u2}_{(16,2)}$ operators. We investigated the accuracy of classification using individual LBP operators to find the best features for efficient classification. Figure 10 shows the plotting of average accuracy of the SVM classifier for determining front and occluded face using different LBP operators. From the graph, it is clear that $LBP^{u2}_{(8,2)}$ operator results in a higher accuracy than other LBP operators, and sigma value of 6.0 gives highest classification accuracy. Therefore, we extracted features using $LBP^{u2}_{(8,2)}$ operators. Table 1 shows the classification rate (%) using different LBP operators with different values of sigma, for identifying the front face and occluded face. In our work the occlusion of eyes by glasses was not considered. As the Kinect depth information is low quality sometimes it is difficult to extract the accurate depth information from the Kinect depth images. Thus, considering only the depth information it is quite difficult to identify the occlusion of eyes with glasses. From the detected occluded facial images, occluded region was localized using our proposed method in [34]. Figure 11 depicts an example of a localized occluded area in depth images (occluded by hand and paper) after correcting the boundary of the occluded region. After localizing the occluded region using our proposed method we visually inspected the localized area. Figure 12 shows the localized region of occlusion (occluded by hand and paper) in the RGB facial images.

Table 1. Classification rate (%) using different LBP operators.

Operator	Feature vector length	Classification rate (%)	Value of sigma
$LBP^{u2}_{(8,1)}$	59	97.25	4.5
$LBP^{u2}_{(8,2)}$	59	98.50	6.0
$LBP^{u2}_{(16,2)}$	243	96.75	9.0

After localizing the occluded area, we extracted the non-occluded region from the facial images. Features are extracted from these non-occluded regions using

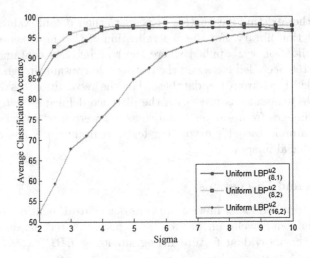

Fig. 10. Plotting of accuracy for different LBP operators.

$LBP_{(8,2)}^{u2}$ operator. The feature vectors are then fed to a KNN classifier for determining the face recognition performance. For simplicity of the implementation, we consider KNN for the recognition task. Table 2 shows the Rank-1 identification rate for the 2D face recognition in the presence of occlusion. The images contain occlusion of mouth by hand and occlusion of face by paper. From the table, we can see that the average identification rate for occlusion of mouth by hand images from the two sessions is 90.39% and the average identification rate for occlusion of face by paper is 83.66%. Table 3 shows the Rank-1 identification rate for the 2D face recognition in the presence of occlusion using our proposed method. For the images containing occlusion of mouth, the average identification rate improves to 95.19%, and for the images containing occlusion of face by paper, the average identification rate improves to 89.42%. Therefore, the proposed face recognition technique improves the recognition performance by using the depth information from the Kinect depth images. The proposed method exploits the depth information for localizing the occluded area in the facial images and discard the occluded area while matching the probe images to the gallery images.

Table 2. Rank-1 identification rate for 2D face recognition under occlusion.

Session	Occlusion by hand	Occlusion by paper
Session 1	92.31%	84.62%
Session 2	88.46%	82.69%

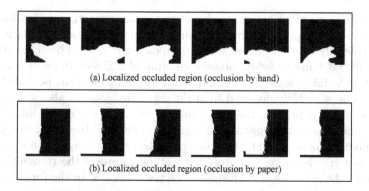

Fig. 11. Example of localized occluded area in the depth images (a) occluded by hand, and (b) occluded by paper.

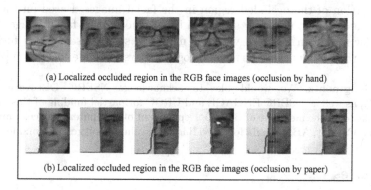

Fig. 12. Example of localized occluded area in the RGB facial images (red marked area), (a) occluded by hand, and (b) occluded by paper (the resolution of the images are 64 × 64). (Color figure online)

Table 3. Rank-1 identification rate For 2D face recognition using proposed method under occlusion.

Session	Occlusion by hand	Occlusion by paper
Session 1	96.15%	90.38%
Session 2	94.23%	88.46%

5 Conclusion

Face recognition under occlusion is one of the active research topics in face automation and security surveillance. In this paper, we present a face recognition technique that will use the depth information acquired using Kinect RGB-D camera for localizing the occluded region from the facial images and use only the non-occluded regions while identifying the user from the gallery images. Local features are extracted from the depth images using LBP operators and a nonlinear SVM classifier is used to detect the front face and occluded face. For localizing occluded regions in the facial image, a threshold based approach is presented to identify the occluded area. The proposed method has been investigated on EUROKOM Kinect face database consisting of different types of occlusions and neutral facial images [20]. Experimental results show that occluded facial images can be effectively detected from the depth images, and also we can localize the occluded regions of the facial images by using the depth information. The recognition system discards the occluded regions of the facial images and match only the non-occluded facial part with the gallery images to find the best possible match. Therefore, the proposed method improves the recognition performance in the presence of occlusion in the facial images. In the future, we will consider other types of occlusions, such as occlusion induced by wearing glasses, hat or other accessories, head rotation and occlusion of different facial parts. We will also estimate the quality of the facial image under occlusion by determining the proportion of the occluded region in the facial images. Based on the ratio of the occluded area, a quality score can be assigned to the facial image. Then, the quality score can be fused with the matching score at score level fusion to determine the confidence of the facial recognition system under occlusion [29, 30].

Acknowledgments. We would like to acknowledge NSERC Discovery Grant RT731064, as well as NSERC ENGAGE and URGC for partial funding of this project. Our thanks to all the members of BTLab, Department of Computer Science, University of Calgary, Calgary, AB, Canada for providing their valuable suggestions and feedback.

References

1. Alyüz, N., Gökberk, B., Spreeuwers, L., Veldhuis, R., Akarun, L.: Robust 3D face recognition in the presence of realistic occlusions. In: 5th IAPR IEEE International Conference on Biometrics (ICB), pp. 111–118, March 2012
2. Canavan, S., Liu, P., Zhang, X., Yin, L.: Landmark localization on 3D/4D range data using a shape index-based statistical shape model with global and local constraints. Comput. Vis. Image Underst. **139**, 136–148 (2015)
3. Cardia Neto, J.B., Marana, A.N.: 3DLBP and HAOG fusion for face recognition utilizing Kinect as a 3D scanner. In: Proceedings of the 30th Annual ACM Symposium on Applied Computing, pp. 66–73. ACM, April 2015
4. Chen, Y.C., Patel, V.M., Phillips, P.J., Chellappa, R.: Dictionary-based face and person recognition from unconstrained video. IEEE Access **3**, 1783–1798 (2015)
5. Colombo, A., Cusano, C., Schettini, R.: Recognizing faces in 3d images even in presence of occlusions. In: 2nd IEEE International Conference on Biometrics: Theory, Applications and Systems, BTAS, pp. 1–6, September 2008
6. Cortes, C., Vapnik, V.: Support-vector networks. Mach. Learn. **20**(3), 273–297 (1995)
7. Drira, H., Ben Amor, B., Srivastava, A., Daoudi, M., Slama, R.: 3D face recognition under expressions, occlusions, and pose variations. IEEE Trans. Pattern Anal. Mach. Intell. **35**(9), 2270–2283 (2013)

8. Forczmański, P., Łabędź, P.: Improving the recognition of occluded faces by means of two-dimensional orthogonal projection into local subspaces. In: Kamel, M., Campilho, A. (eds.) ICIAR 2015. LNCS, vol. 9164, pp. 229–238. Springer, Cham (2015). doi:10.1007/978-3-319-20801-5_25

9. Ganguly, S., Bhattacharjee, D., Nasipuri, M.: Depth based occlusion detection and localization from 3D face image. Int. J. Image Graph. Sig. Process. **7**(5), 20–31 (2015)

10. Gul, S., Farooq, H.: A machine learning approach to detect occluded faces in unconstrained crowd scene. In: 14th International Conference on Cognitive Informatics & Cognitive Computing (ICCI* CC), pp. 149–155. IEEE, July 2015

11. Hassaballah, M., Aly, S.: Face recognition: challenges, achievements and future directions. IET Comput. Vis. **9**(4), 614–626 (2015)

12. Henry, P., Krainin, M., Herbst, E., Ren, X., Fox, D.: RGB-D mapping: using Kinect-style depth cameras for dense 3D modeling of indoor environments. Int. J. Robot. Res. **31**(5), 647–663 (2012)

13. Hsu, G.S.J., Liu, Y.L., Peng, H.C., Wu, P.X.: RGB-D-based face reconstruction and recognition. IEEE Trans. Inf. Forensics Secur. **9**(12), 2110–2118 (2014)

14. Izadi, S., Kim, D., Hilliges, O., Molyneaux, D., Newcombe, R., Kohli, P., Shotton, J., Hodges, S., Freeman, D., Davison, A., Fitzgibbon, A.: KinectFusion: real-time 3D reconstruction and interaction using a moving depth camera. In: Proceedings of the 24th Annual ACM Symposium on User Interface Software and Technology, pp. 559–568. ACM, October 2011

15. Jain, A.K., Nandakumar, K., Ross, A.: 50 years of biometric research: accomplishments, challenges, and opportunities. Pattern Recogn. Lett. **79**, 80–105 (2016)

16. Johnson, R., O'Hara, K., Sellen, A., Cousins, C., Criminisi, A.: Exploring the potential for touchless interaction in image-guided interventional radiology. In: Proceedings of the SIGCHI Conference on Human Factors in Computing Systems, pp. 3323–3332. ACM, May 2011

17. KONICA Minolta. http://www.konicaminolta.com/. Accessed 03 Feb 2016

18. Li, X.X., Dai, D.Q., Zhang, X.F., Ren, C.X.: Structured sparse error coding for face recognition with occlusion. IEEE Trans. Image Process. **22**(5), 1889–1900 (2013)

19. Liao, S., Jain, A., Li, S.: A fast and accurate unconstrained face detector. IEEE Trans. Pattern Anal. Mach. Intell. **38**(2), 211–223 (2016)

20. Min, R., Kose, N., Dugelay, J.L.: KinectFaceDB: A Kinect database for face recognition. IEEE Trans. Syst. Man Cybern. Syst. **44**(11), 1534–1548 (2014)

21. Ojala, T., Pietikäinen, M., Mäenpää, T.: Multiresolution gray-scale and rotation invariant texture classification with local binary patterns. IEEE Trans. Pattern Anal. Mach. Intell. **24**(7), 971–87 (2002)

22. Ojala, T., Pietikäinen, M., Mäenpää, T.: A generalized Local Binary Pattern operator for multiresolution gray scale and rotation invariant texture classification. In: ICAPR, vol. 1, pp. 397–406, March 2001

23. Ouloul, M.I., Moutakki, Z., Afdel, K., Amghar, A.: An efficient face recognition using SIFT descriptor in RGB-D images. Int. J. Electr. Comput. Eng. **5**(6), 1227–1233 (2015)

24. Phillips, P.J., Flynn, P.J., Scruggs, T., Bowyer, K.W., Chang, J., Hoffman, K., Marques, J., Min, J., Worek, W.: Overview of the face recognition grand challenge. In: IEEE Computer Society Conference on Computer Vision and Pattern Recognition, CVPR 2005, vol. 1, pp. 947–954, June 2005

25. Saxena, A., Chung, S.H., Ng, A.Y.: 3-d depth reconstruction from a single still image. Int. J. Comput. Vis. **76**(1), 53–69 (2008)

26. Shao, L., Han, J., Xu, D., Shotton, J.: Computer vision for RGB-D sensors: Kinect and its applications. IEEE Trans. Cybern. **43**(5), 1314–1317 (2013)
27. Shotton, J., Sharp, T., Kipman, A., Fitzgibbon, A., Finocchio, M., Blake, A., Cook, M., Moore, R.: Real-time human pose recognition in parts from single depth images. Commun. ACM **56**(1), 116–124 (2013)
28. Srinivasan, A., Balamurugan, V.: Occlusion detection and image restoration in 3D face image. In: TENCON IEEE Region 10 Conference, pp. 1–6, October 2014
29. Sultana, M., Gavrilova, M., Alhajj, R., Yanushkevich, S.: Adaptive multi-stream score fusion for illumination invariant face recognition. In: IEEE Symposium on Computational Intelligence in Biometrics and Identity Management (CIBIM), pp. 94–101, December 2014
30. Sultana, M., Gavrilova, M., Yanushkevich, S.: Fuzzy rule based quality measures for adaptive multimodal biometric fusion at operation time. In: IJCCI, 6th International Conference on Fuzzy Computation Theory and Applications (FCTA), pp. 146–152 (2014)
31. Vapnik, V.N.: An overview of statistical learning theory. IEEE Trans. Neural Networks **10**(5), 988–999 (1999)
32. Viola, P., Jones, M.: Rapid object detection using a boosted cascade of simple features. In: Proceedings of the 2001 IEEE Computer Society Conference on Computer Vision and Pattern Recognition, CVPR 2001, vol. 1, p. I-511 (2001)
33. Xia, Y., Zhang, B., Coenen, F.: Face occlusion detection based on multi-task convolution neural network. In: 12th International Conference on Fuzzy Systems and Knowledge Discovery (FSKD), pp. 375–379. IEEE, August 2015
34. Zohra, F.T., Rahman, M.W., Gavrilova, M.: Occlusion detection and localization from kinect depth images. In: International Conference on Cyberworlds (CW), pp. 189–196. IEEE (2016)

Scene-Aware Style Transferring Using GIST

Masahiro Toyoura, Noriyuki Abe, and Xiaoyang Mao[✉]

University of Yamanashi, Kofu, Yamanashi, Japan
mao@yamanashi.ac.jp

Abstract. This paper proposes a new method of transferring style between images by considering scene matching between the source image and the target image. Artists often employ different colors and brushwork for individual subjects. Likewise, the connections between various subjects in a work also affect the colors and brushwork used. Our method begins with input images, searches an example database for paintings with scenes similar to that in the input image, and transfers the color and brushwork of the paintings to the corresponding target images to generate painterly images that reflect specific styles. Our method applies a GIST approach to the process of searching for paintings with similar scenes before performing style transfers. The spatial correspondence between the source image and the target image is also used to ensure close correlation between various elements in order to reproduce styles faithfully.

1 Introduction

Painting is a challenge for most people. In the past decade, many commercial or free image processing software have been developed allowing users to create painterly images with ease. In most cases, however, these types of software simply process the entire input image with some kind of filter and the end result is thus usually far removed from the look of an actual painting. More sophisticated filtering algorithms, using modern computer vision and image processing techniques, have been developed to create various stylized images [9]. However, the representation that can be created by those techniques is inherently limited to an abstraction of some particular style. Working to generate painterly images that more closely resemble real paintings, researchers have conducted physical simulations of various painting materials and painting methods, such as colored pencils, watercolors, and ink, among others [7]. Using these techniques to create painterly images requires making adjustments to a vast array of different parameters, such as pen tip shape, brush pressure, pigment viscosity, and translucency. A user thus often needs to know not only how to use the software in question but also how to do the actual painting.

Recently, an example-based approach that uses learning technology to transfer the artistic style of an example work onto an arbitrary image is attracting a large amount of attention [2,5,17]. While the filtering or physical simulation-based approaches usually encode a set of heuristics to mimic or simulate particular predefined styles, the largest advantage of the example-based approach

© Springer-Verlag GmbH Germany 2017
M.L. Gavrilova et al. (Eds.): Trans. on Comput. Sci. XXX, LNCS 10560, pp. 29–49, 2017.
https://doi.org/10.1007/978-3-662-56006-8_3

is that it applies to any style in principle given the example image in the style. The majority of example-based painterly image generation techniques apply texture synthesis technology for transferring the appearance of the brush strokes in the example painting onto a target image. As style of brush stroke is one of the main attributes contributing to a unique painting style, such approaches have high potential to generate painterly images reflecting the style of individual artists.

Turn one's eye to real paintings, however, and artists usually use different colors and brush strokes for different objects. Even the same subjects may be painted differently based on where the subjects are and what else is in the scene. Therefore, transferring a style from a painting depicting a completely different scene may fail to reproduce the intended style. One such example is shown in Fig. 1. The results are obtained by applying Image Analogies, a well-known example-based technique proposed by Hertzmann et al. [8], to transfer the texture of the brush stroke from the reference painting to the input photograph. The stroke texture of the white German iris in the painting was transferred into the sky in the photograph because of the similarities in color and position of the two subjects, resulting in the unnatural depiction of the sky. The example shows the importance of the correspondence of subjects and compositions between the source painting and the target image.

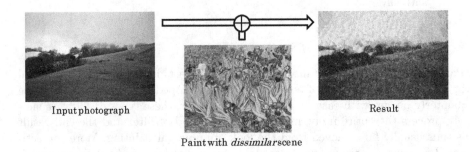

Input photograph   Result

Paint with *dissimilar* scene

Fig. 1. Transferring style from a painting with a *dissimilar* scene.

In this paper, we propose a new scene-aware style transferring technique to automatically generate painterly images. Given an input image, our method first searches the example painting database for a painting depicting a similar scene and then transfers the color and texture between the corresponding regions of the painting and the input image. Establishing perfect correspondence between the elements of two images requires comprehensive understanding of the contents of the image, which cannot be achieved even with the most advanced computer vision technologies. Fortunately, it is known that artists, especially the majority of impressionists, are likely to paint a scene perceptually without constructing a semantical model of the scene. Based on this assumption, we combine a GIST feature [6], which describes the overall composition of a scene as initially perceived by a human, normally within 100 msec of seeing an image or scenery, with a color feature for searching for paintings of similar scenes. The result generated by applying the proposed method to the photograph is shown in Fig. 2. The algorithm first obtained painting with a similar scene from the example painting database and then transferred the color and texture of this painting to the input image by considering the local correspondence between the two images. Compared with the synthesized result image in Fig. 1, the result in Fig. 2 appears to better reflect the style of the original painting. We have conducted subject studies to evaluate the effectiveness of our new painting retrieval technique and we investigate whether the proposed technique can generate painterly images that well preserve the styles of the example paintings.

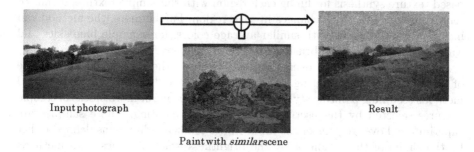

Input photograph   Result

Paint with *similar* scene

Fig. 2. Transferring style from a painting with a *similar* scene.

Our major contributions can be summarized as follows:

(1) The novel idea of introducing a scene-aware approach to the texture synthesis–based style transferring method.
(2) Improvements to the conventional GIST-based image retrieval method by incorporating color feature and local distance.
(3) The new scene-aware style transferring algorithm obtained by adding position-based constraints to the existing color and texture transfer technique.

The remainder of this paper is organized as follows: Sect. 2 reviews related works from the literature. After giving an overview of the proposed method in Sect. 3, Sect. 4 presents the technique for searching for paintings with similar scenes. Section 5 describes the algorithm for transferring styles. Section 6 explains the results of the conducted experiments, and Sect. 7 concludes the paper.

2   Related Works

Image Analogies [8], mentioned in the Introduction, is a pioneering work of example-based style transferring techniques. The method learns the mapping between an exemplar pair: a source image and an artist's rendering of that image. The learned mapping can then be applied to render arbitrary images in the exemplar style. As depicted in Fig. 1, although Image Analogies provided an elegant framework for learning arbitrary artistic style using non-parametric texture synthesis, it may fail to reproduce the desired style if the scene depicted by the painting and the scene captured by the photograph are too different. Our proposed method employs Image Analogies for local texture transferring but ensure the quality of the result by finding a matching painting and performing scene aware transferring. Chang et al. [2] used the mean-shift method to divide the input image and paintings into color-specific regions. A region of a sample painting is cropped to a rectangular patch and used as the sample texture for the region with similar average color in the input image. As the method uses patch-based texture synthesis for filling each region with the sample texture, it fails to represent the subtle tone changes in each region. Furthermore, the method can incorrectly link regions with similar average colors, for example blue skies and water, which should have brush strokes with different feels.

Several methods have been proposed to learn the directional appearance of brush strokes in a painting. Wang et al. [2,17] and Guo et al. [5] proposed methods assuming painting styles are represented as one or more blocks of sample textures selected by the user from the example painting. Those samples are superimposed over regions of the input image following directions defined either by the shape of the region or by the brightness gradient. These two methods require the user to specify regions manually and the quality of the resulting image may depend on the user's skill.

Lee et al. [10,11] extended Ashikhmin's fast texture synthesis technique [1] to generate directional effect in the resulting image. Either in Image Analogies or Ashikhmin's algorithm, two different searches are combined to find the best matching pixels. One is an approximate search that attempts to find the closest-matching pixel according to the neighborhoods in the source image and the other is a coherence search that attempts to preserve coherence with the neighboring synthesized pixels in the resulting image. Lee et al.'s method generates the directional effect by adding a third coherence search item which search for the pixel in the source image with small difference from the average value of the pixels along the direction perpendicular to the gradient of the resulting image. Since the directional effect is produced by favoring the coherence in the resulting image along a particular direction, their method may fail to transfer the original filtering effect.

Xie et al. [18,19] also tackled to improve the quality of the resulting image by trying to better preserve the structure information in the synthesized image. They proposed to adaptively vary the coherence parameter according to their distance from the structural features such edges and boundaries. Chang et al. [3] proposed to adaptively changing the patch size when performing patch based texture synthesis. Lee et al. [12] tried to improve the quality of texture synthesis by using the structure information in similarity searching. Same as in the very basic Image Analogies technique, all of these methods perform texture transfer without aware of the scene correspondence between the example painting and the input image. Our technique can be easily combined with those sophisticated texture transferring method for achieving more impressive results.

The above–mentioned style transferring approaches mainly rely on non-parametric techniques to directly manipulate the pixel representation of an image. Gatys et al. [4] attempted to use deep neural networks to carry out manipulations in feature spaces that explicitly represent the high–level content of an image. The feature space is built on top of the filter responses in multiple layers of the network. Then, by mixing the higher layer of the input image and the lower layers of the example images, they succeeded in generating results that present the content of the input image in the style of the example input image. Although several plausible results are shown in [4], the selection of appropriate layers in the multi-scale feature spaces can be image dependent and difficult.

However, the idea of combining data–driven approaches with the rich data resources of the web has attracted a great deal of attention. Liu et al. [14] proposed a technique that stylizes a user's photo by transferring style from a collection of images returned by a web search for a particular keyword. However, their methods mainly focus on transferring color and contrast, and the expected results can be obtained only when the retrieved images have attached keywords matching the image style.

As a content–aware approach, Shih et al. [16] developed a technique for transferring style between headshot portraits. Their method establishes the correspondence between the local features of the example stylized portrait and the target photograph and robustly transfers the local statistics from the example image to the target image. However, their technique is tailored for portraits and cannot be applied to other photographs.

3   Overview

Figure 3 shows a schematic overview of our method, which comprises the example painting database construction and runtime painterly image generation stages. To construct the database, feature vectors for describing the scene depicted by each painting example are computed and stored together with the paintings. The examples are divided into different sets by artist name, materials, and techniques. At runtime, the user inputs an image and keywords (artist name, materials, and/or techniques). The system then computes the scene feature vector for the input image and uses the feature vector to search the corresponding image set in the database for a painting that depicts a similar scene as the input image. Upon finding a similar painting, the system transfers the color and brushwork from the painting to the input image to generate a painterly image. The details of each step of the algorithm are introduced in the following sections.

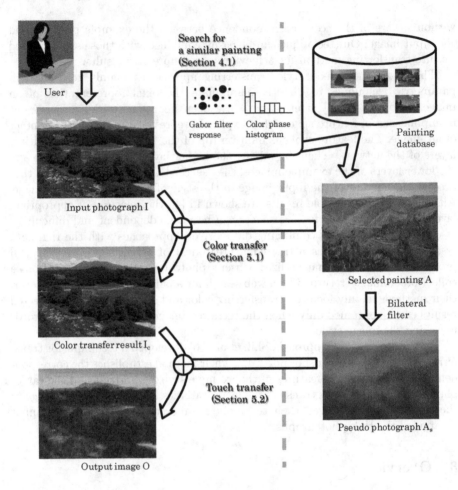

Fig. 3. Overview of our proposed method.

4   Searching for Paintings with Similar Scenes

Composition and color are two main elements that help to determine the similarity of two scenes. The GIST feature, which models the rapid initial recognition of human visual perception, is an effective gauge of a scene's composition. We combine a GIST feature with a color feature to automatically select from a sample painting set a painting that depicts a scene similar to the scene in the input picture.

4.1   Feature Vector

GIST. GIST perception is the visual perception that a human experiences within 100 ms of seeing an image or scenery. In this perceptional period, humans can recognize the overall composition of what they are looking at. Oliva and Torralba [15] proposed the following multidirectional, multifrequency Gabor filter banks that could be used as a computational model for GIST: Passing an image through Gabor filters gives the viewer a basic idea of the shapes of the subjects in the image. Formula 1 is the formula for Oliva and Torralba's multidirectional, multifrequency Gabor filters.

$$g(x, y : \lambda, \theta, \psi, \sigma, \gamma)$$
$$= \exp(-\frac{x'^2 + \gamma^2 y'^2}{2\sigma^2}) \sin(2\pi\frac{x'}{\lambda} + \psi), \tag{1}$$
$$x' = x\cos\theta + y\sin\theta, \ y' = x\sin\theta + y\cos\theta.$$

Here, λ is the frequency parameter. Controlling this value makes it possible to create Gabor filters for various frequencies. θ is the parameter for direction, the control of which makes it possible to create Gabor filters with different orientations. Figure 4 shows the results of passing an image through multidirectional, multifrequency Gabor filters.

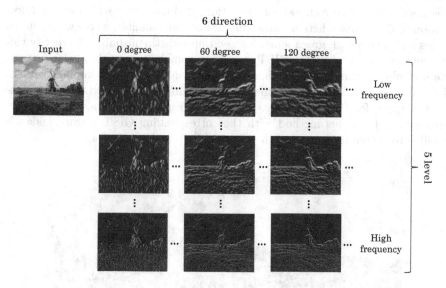

Fig. 4. Structure information obtained via multidirectional, multiresolutional Gabor filters.

A low-frequency Gabor filter reacts to and detects the larger, wider structures in the image, while a high-frequency Gabor filter reacts to and detects the smaller, finer structures in the image. The filter also detects structures extending in specific directions, depending on the angle. The GIST feature is calculated by applying multidirectional, multifrequency Gabor flters to the image, dividing the results from each filter into a grid of regions, and computing the sum of each region. Such a GIST feature represents the composition of an image or view and provides a general structure of the subjects in each region. The method proposed in this paper involves passing the input image through a total of 30 Gabor filters (six directions at five frequency levels) to compute the GIST feature. GIST feature quantity is usually calculated by applying multidirectional, multiresolutional Gabor filters to the image, dividing the results from each filter into a grid of regions, and finding the sum of each region. The GIST feature has been primarily used in performing high-speed searches of large-scale image databases for images with similar compositions. Hoping to interpolate partially damaged images, Hays and Efros [6] achieved some good results using a GIST feature to search the massive volume of images available on the Internet for images with compositions similar to that of an input image. There are many other cases where GIST has helped researchers rapidly sift through the innumerable images on the Internet to find and use images with similar compositions.

Color. Users can use a GIST feature to get a basic idea of the structure of the subjects in an image and then search for an image with similar composition. However, these features are generally based on image edge information. While this allows for image composition detection, it does not provide enough information to determine whether two scenes are actually similar; a tree with colored leaves and a tree with green leaves can end up indistinguishable. To rectify this problem, our method uses a GIST feature in combination with a color feature. We use color feature corresponding to a histogram of the hue component of the HSV color model. We quantize the hue wheel into 12 equal parts and compute the histogram for the input image as shown in Fig. 5. Combining the color feature obtained via this method with the corresponding GIST feature makes it possible to search for images with perceptually matching scenes.

(a) Input image   (b) Results of quantizing the image
                              into 12 colors using color phases

Fig. 5. Image quantized into 12 colors using color phases. (Color figure online)

4.2   The Rule of Thirds

The above discussion examined the methods for calculating the GIST feature and color feature. These features are computed by passing an image through filters, dividing the resulting image into a grid, and then adding up the corresponding pixel values in individual regions. Oliva and Torralba [15] used a 4 × 4 grid to compute the GIST feature. For the method proposed in this paper, we use the "rule of thirds," a classic technique in the artistic disciplines, based on the consideration that the images to be searched for are artistic works. The rule of thirds, used to compose paintings, pictures, and other visual images, proposes that an image should be divided by two equally spaced horizontal lines and two equally spaced vertical lines. The boundaries between land and sky, etc., in the image should be placed along these lines, and the most important subjects should be situated on the intersections between the lines. The Monet painting shown in Fig. 6(a) is an illustration of the rule of thirds. The boundary between the water and sky aligns with a horizontal dividing line, while the important subjects – the yacht and the house – lie where the lines cross. This placement guideline stabilizes the composition, creating a more attractive paintings or picture. The rule of thirds has also been used as a criterion for a compositional placement optimization technique designed to improve the aesthetic quality of a painting (Liu et al. [13]). The method proposed in this paper adopts the rule of thirds to create nine block regions, divided by equally spaced horizontal and vertical lines, when calculating the GIST feature and color feature. As the boundaries

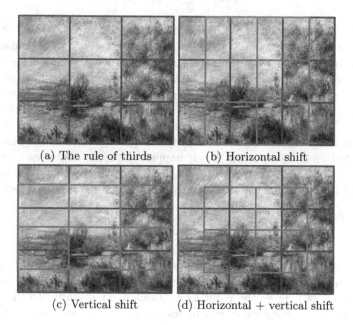

(a) The rule of thirds   (b) Horizontal shift

(c) Vertical shift   (d) Horizontal + vertical shift

Fig. 6. Rule of thirds–based composition.

and objects tend to fall on these lines, we shift phases and use block regions containing lines to capture this information (Fig. 6(b) and (c)). The important subjects in an image also tend to lie on the intersections between the lines representing the rule of thirds. Information about these objects can be captured by using block regions that contain these intersections, which can be obtained by shifting phases both vertically and horizontally as shown in Fig. 6(d). In summary, our method calculates the GIST and color features based on 25 total block regions: the 9 block regions created by breaking the image into a 3 × 3 grid and the 16 regions created by shifting phases to include the lines and intersections of the rule of thirds.

The feature calculation is performed after normalizing the sizes of paintings. Using the results of passing the image through the Gabor filter and the results of quantizing the image into 12 colors, the method then calculates the GIST feature and color feature of each of the 25 block regions to produce a feature vector with 1,050 dimensions ((6 directions × 5 frequency levels + 12 colors) × 25 block regions).

4.3   Distance

We evaluate the similarity of the scenes of input image i and the searched painting s using the following global distance $G_{g(i,s)}$.

$$G_{g(i,s)} = \sum_{n=1}^{25} |F_n^i - F_n^s|. \tag{2}$$

Here, $|\cdot|$ expresses the L_2 norm, while F_n^i and F_n^s are the 42-dimension (6 directions × 5 frequency levels + 12 colors) feature vectors for the image i and painting s, respectively. However, this formula is not ideal. Imagine, for instance, two scenes depicting cars. Provided that there are no major differences in the backgrounds, a person would think the scenes are essentially the same even if the cars are in slightly different positions. If the positions of the cars in the images are at least 1 block different, Eq. (2) would produce a large distance value and classify the images as dissimilar. To rectify this problem, our method introduces a component that incorporates local mapping into the distance: it compares regions that are the most similar rather than regions in the same positions. This component is called the local distance value G_l and is expressed as follows:

$$G_{l(i,s)} = \sum_{n=1}^{25} \min_{m} |F_n^i - F_m^s|. \tag{3}$$

F_m^s represents the region with the feature vector that most closely approximates region F_n^i in the input image. Independent of position, Eq. (3) produces a small distance value as long as the painting contains regions similar to those of the picture. As the resulting value will be low in any case where two images have similar elements, using this local distance by itself creates the risk of returning a search result with a completely different composition. Thus, our method calculates a final difference value G as the weighted sum of the global distance in Eq. (2) and the local distance in Eq. (3) in order to measure the similarity in terms of both composition and elements.

$$G_{(i,s)} = (1.0 - \rho)G_{g(i,s)} + \rho G_{l(i,s)}. \tag{4}$$

One can change the focus between composition and elements by modifying coefficient $\rho(0.0 \leq \rho \leq 1.0)$. Increasing ρ makes the search procedure more likely to return a painting with the same sorts of subjects as the picture, even if the scenes are different.

As local distance values are calculated using the most similar regions from the two images, the theoretical range may be the same as that of the global distance value, but the actual value will be much smaller. In order to ensure the effectiveness of Eq. (4) in an actual usage setting, our method uses statistical methods to predict and normalize the actual ranges of both distance values. After calculating the averages and distributions of the local and global distances for the input image and all the painting images in the painting database, the method uses Eqs. (5) and (6) to normalize both distance values to within the range of 0.0 to 1.0.

$$G'_{g(i,s)} = \frac{1}{1 + exp(-(G_{g(i,s)} - \bar{G}_g)/\sigma_{Gg})}, \tag{5}$$

$$G'_{l(i,s)} = \frac{1}{1 + exp(-(G_{l(i,s)} - \bar{G}_l)/\sigma_{Gl})}. \tag{6}$$

Here, $G'_g(i, s)$ and $G'_l(i, s)$ are the normalized local distance and global distance, respectively. $\bar{G}_g$ and $\bar{G}_l$ are the statistically calculated averages of the respective distance, while σ_{G_g} and σ_{G_l} are the respective distributions. In our method, we calculate these values for every input image and normalize accordingly based on the pictures. The method then uses distance, calculated by replacing $G_g(i, s)$ and $G_l(i, s)$ from Eq. (4) with $G'_{g(i,s)}$ and $G'_{l(i,s)}$ from Eqs. (5) and (6), to measure the similarity of the images' compositions and elements.

5   Transferring Painting Features

The painting used for feature transfer purposes shares a similar composition with the picture in question, so there is a good chance that both images will feature similar elements in corresponding positions. Given this assumption, our method takes position linking into account when transferring features. Before transferring color, we remap the colors to align the overall color of input image i with that of example painting s. Color remapping is performed using Eq. (7). Here, color is the pixel value of each component of input image i in YIQ color space; σ_i and σ_s are the standard deviations of each component of the input image and example painting, respectively; and $\bar{i}$ and $\bar{s}$ are the averages of each component of the input image and example painting, respectively.

$$color' = \frac{\sigma_s}{\sigma_i}(color - \bar{i}) + \bar{s}. \tag{7}$$

5.1 Transferring Color

Color transferring is done by setting the color of a pixel p in input image i to that of the pixel q that has the smallest distance $C(i, s, p, q)$ from p among all other pixels in painting s. The distance $C(i, s, p, q)$ is given by Eq. (8). ΔEab is the color distance in $L^*a^*b^*$ color space between p and q, and σ is the standard deviation of the brightness in their neighborhood. The differences of both the color and brightness deviation are divided by the available maximum to normalize them within the range of 0.0 to 1.0.

$$C_{(i,s,p,q)} = (1 - \gamma)(\frac{\Delta Eab}{2} + \frac{|\sigma_p - \sigma_q|}{2}) + \gamma \Delta F_{l(i,s,p,q)}, \tag{8}$$

$$\Delta F_{l(i,s,p,q)} = |F_p^i - F_q^s|.$$

The third term $\Delta F_{l(i,s,p,q)}$ is the local distance measuring the similarity between the block regions consisting of pixel p in input image i and pixel q in painting s. It is computed as the L_2 norm of the 42-dimension GIST and color feature vector of the two regions. Because $\Delta F_{l(i,s,p,q)}$ is computed for each region, discontinuity can be observed at the boundaries between two regions. To solve this problem and prevent $\Delta F_{l(i,s,p,q)}$ from changing suddenly at region boundaries, our method computes $\Delta F_{l(i,s,p,q)}$ through the bi-linear interpolation of its values at the four surrounding block regions. As shown in Fig. 7, we denote the four surrounding closest regions as LT, RT, LB, and RB and the distance from the pixel to the center of each block as D_T, D_L, D_R, and D_B, respectively, from which $\Delta F_{(i,s,p,q)}$ can be computed with Eq. (9).

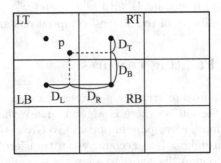

Fig. 7. Bilinear interpolation of region difference.

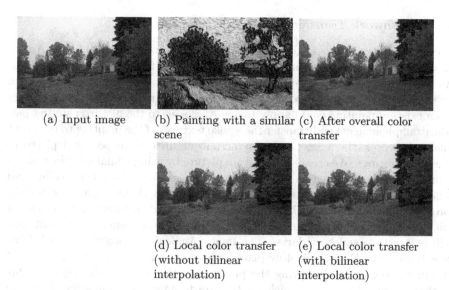

(a) Input image   (b) Painting with a similar (c) After overall color
                    scene   transfer

(d) Local color transfer   (e) Local color transfer
(without bilinear   (with bilinear
interpolation)   interpolation)

Fig. 8. Color transfer results. (Color figure online)

$$\Delta F_{l(i,s)} = (D_L \ D_R) \begin{pmatrix} |F_p^{iLT} - F_q^s| & |F_p^{iLB} - F_q^s| \\ |F_p^{iRT} - F_q^s| & |F_p^{iRB} - F_q^s| \end{pmatrix} \begin{pmatrix} D_T \\ D_B \end{pmatrix}. \tag{9}$$

In Eq. (8), a constant $r(0.0 \leq r \leq 1.0)$ is used to control the weight of color and brightness distribution over the GIST feature and can be specified by the user. Figure 8 shows the color transfer results. Figure 8(c) shows the results generated when the overall color of the painting in Fig. 8(b) was remapped onto the picture in Fig. 8(a) using Eq. (7). Figure 8(d) shows the results generated by transferring the color of pixels in Fig. 8(b) with the smallest distance given by Eq. (8) without considering the discontinuity at the boundaries. Figure 8(e) shows the results when using bilinear interpolation to compute $\Delta F_{(i,s,p,q)}$. The predominant red tones of Fig. 8(b) were transferred to Fig. 8(c), making the trees with slightly colored leaves look red. Considering that there are no red trees in the painting, however, the process of transferring the style of the painting should not result in the production of red trees. For Fig. 8(d) and (e), the color from Fig. 8(b) was transferred in a more detailed manner by including the cost of local distance. We can see that the trees that were red in the last comparison have turned green and now bear the color of the trees in the painting. The sky also features yellow, bringing it closer to the color of the sky in the painting. Figure 8(d) does not use interpolation and therefore shows sharp changes at regional boundaries, creating discontinuity in the transfer of the sky colors. Meanwhile, the discontinuity is eliminated in Fig. 8(e) because the use of biliear interpolation prevents marked changes in feature similarity near boundaries.

5.2   Brushwork Transfer

Our method uses Image Analogies [8] for brushwork transfer. With Image Analogies, one can transfer the relationship between texture features in example images A and A' to B and then create B', an image with the same relationship between texture features. In other words, a user with a picture of a scene that appears in an existing painting could apply Image Analogies to the picture painting pair (the example images) and transfer the stroke textures of the painting to the input image. However, there are rarely any actual pictures of the scenes depicted in existing paintings. We create a substitute picture by using a bilateral filter on the source painting. As painters often use brushstrokes to evoke various colors and tones, regions of pictures where colors and brightness change in a smooth fashion sometimes also contain high-frequency stroke texture components. Using a bilateral filter, one can eliminate these in-region high-frequency components but still protect regional boundaries. The Image Analogies approach copies brightness from A' to B on a pixel-by-pixel basis, comparing the colors of A and B in window regions and copying the pixels from the most similar regions. Our method brings $\Delta F_{l(i,s,p,q)}$, which Eq. (9) uses to gauge the similarity of feature vectors across regions, into this operation. The following formula is used to calculate distance $S_{(i,s,p,q)}$, which figures into the transfer of pixel q from painting s to pixel p of input image i.

$$S_{(i,s,p,q)} = (1 - \gamma)(|W_p^B - W_q^A| + |W_p^{B'} - W_q^{A'}|) + \gamma \Delta F_{l(i,s)}. \qquad (10)$$

Here, W_qs and W_ss are the window regions around the pixels p and q, respectively, and $\Delta F_{l(i,s,p,q)}$ is the local distance and is the same as for Eq. (8). For the transfer to pixel p, the method finds the pixel q with the smallest $S(i, s, p, q)$ in Eq. (10) and transfers the Y value of pixel q in YIQ color space to pixel p.

6   Results and Experiments

6.1   Results

We used Google Images to search for paintings by 12 different painters, including Van Gogh and Monet, using the search string "(painter name)" and "landscape-photo." We retrieved approximately 500 images of paintings and stored them in a database together with the precomputed feature vectors.

Figures 9 and 10 show several results generated with the proposed method. The left column shows the input pictures. The images shown in the middle column are the paintings automatically retrieved from the database. The right column shows the results obtained by transferring the color and textures of the corresponding paintings to the input pictures. We can see that paintings with similar scenes have been retrieved and their color and brush work styles were successfully transferred to the input images.

6.2   Evaluation

Painting Retrieval with Improved GIST Feature. We conducted a subjective evaluation experiment to determine whether the method proposed in this paper could search the database for images with similar scenes and properly rank the images by similarity. We recruited 12 university students as the subjects. For the experiment, we applied our method to eight pictures with different scenes and searched the database for ranked results of similar painting images. We set the ρ coefficient for weighting local distance and global distance to 0.5. Then, we selected the highest-ranked image search result and 11 other randomly selected search results to create a set of 12 painting images for each picture.

When presenting the 12 painting images to the participants, we randomly shuffled the highest-ranked search result with the 11 other randomly selected search results and displayed all the images simultaneously on a single web page. From these 12 choices, the subjects were asked to select the painting image with the scene that most closely resembles that of the picture. Our null hypothesis was that the 12 painting images would all be chosen with equal probability. Under that hypothesis, we used a binomial test to determine whether the painting image with the highest ranking by the proposed method received a significant number of votes from the subjects. If our method proved to be an effective means of searching for painting images with similar scenes, there would be a statistically significant correlation between the highest-ranking image selected by the system and the images selected by the experiment participants. Table 1 shows the results.

Table 1. The number (and ratio) of people (out of 12 subjects in total) who chose the method's highest-ranking image as the image with the most similar scene (**: $p \leq 0.01$, *: $p \leq 0.05$, +: $p \leq 0.1$).

Dataset	A	B	C	D	E	F	G	H
Number of subjects	3	10	3	8	9	4	1	8
Ratio	0.25^+	0.83^{**}	0.25^+	0.67^{**}	0.75^{**}	0.33^*	0.08	0.67^{**}

The subjects selected the highest-ranking image with statistical significance for 7 of the 8 pictures. These results suggest that, for most pictures, the search method proposed in this paper is capable of retrieving images that are perceptually similar to the picture. The findings also imply that the automatic process of selecting the highest ranking painting image from the database as the transfer source is effective in the majority of cases.

Style Transferring. We also conducted a subjective evaluation experiment to determine whether the method could reflect the styles of specific painters. Example paintings by 12 artists were used in the experiment.

Fig. 9. Results. Left: input images, middle: retrieved example paintings, right: synthe-sized images. Corresponding painters, from top to bottom: (5) Gustave Caillebotte, (7) Jacob Isaacksz van Ruisdael, (8) Jean-Baptiste Armand Guillaumin, and (10) Claude Monet.

(1) Berthe Morisot
(2) Edgar Degas
(3) Eugene Henri Paul Gauguin
(4) Vincent van Gogh
(5) Gustave Caillebotte
(6) Jacob Camille Pissarro
(7) Jacob Isaacksz van Ruisdael
(8) Jean-Baptiste Armand Guillaumin
(9) Jean-Baptiste-Camille Corot

Fig. 10. Results. Left: input images, middle: retrieved example paintings, right: synthesized images. Corresponding painters, from top to bottom, (1) Berthe Morisot, (3) Eugene Henri Paul Gauguin, (4) Vincent van Gogh, and (12) Pierre-Auguste Renoir.

(10) Claude Monet
(11) Paul Cezanne
(12) Pierre-Auguste Renoir

Subjects were shown an image generated by transferring a specific painter's style onto a picture and a set of 12 painting images, including the specific painter's work used for the transfer and 11 other paintings not used as the example painting. The 11 paintings not used as the example (hereafter called reference paintings) were obtained by searching the database for paintings by the other 11 painters and choosing the works that had the strongest similarities with the example painting in terms of both the scene and the painting style. We displayed each of the 12 paintings together with the generated image one at a time for 10 s each in random order. We then explained the concepts of "brushwork" and "color" to the subjects, who proceeded to rate each painting's degree of similarity to the generated image (with 1 being the lowest degree of similarity and 7 being the highest). The subjects are eight university students. Table 2 shows the results of the experiment. We computed the average degree of similarity of the eight subjects for each of the 12 paintings and then used the Wilcoxon signed-rank test to test the presence of any significant difference between the example painting and each of the 11 reference paintings. Table 2 shows the number of paintings with an average degree of similarity significantly lower (at significance level of 5%) than that of the example painting used to generate the image.

Table 2. Number of paintings (out of 11 in total) evaluated as having significantly lower average degree of similarity (at a significance level of 5%) than the example painting.

ID	1	2	3	4	5	6	7	8	9	10	11	12
Vote	7	9	11	11	11	11	9	7	11	11	11	4

Among the 12 images evaluated, 7 images were evaluated to be more similar to the example painting than all 11 of the other reference paintings. Among the remaining 5 images, 2 were evaluated to be more similar to the example painting than 9 of the other paintings and 2 were evaluated to be more similar to the example painting than 7 of the other paintings. Only 1 image was evaluated to be less similar to the example painting than 7 other paintings. The fact that for 5 images, the example image was not always the one selected as most similar does not necessarily mean that the method failed to transfer the style. In some cases, an image by an artist with a style more similar to that of the artist of the example painting was present.

We showed the resulting images to two professional painters. The following are their comments on the three images with the best, worst, and middle scores in Table 2. The images are also shown in Fig. 10.

ID 3 (11 votes): The generated image is good as a painting. Colors are well transferred. The characteristics of Gauguin are not well represented in the image. Fine textures are lost. By blending the generated image and the original input, it may be possible to represent the textures in the result.

ID 1 (7 votes): The result is acceptable though not so good. Coloring and shading look good. The touch is beautiful, but does not resemble that of the original painting. The touch of tiny regions such as woods and small objects is well transferred in the image. Colors are also transferred, but lack depth. The image well reflects the atmosphere of the original painting on the whole. We can feel hazy air in the space.

ID 12 (4 votes): Objects are more vividly colored in the painting than they actually are, but such exaggeration is not achieved in the generated image. The vertical lines are transferred, but not enough. One can see the flow of touch in the original painting, while such effect is not well represented in the generated image. The inconsistency of directions between shadows and touch can be perceived. The aliasing artifacts can be seen on the thin branches of trees. The thinnest ones are not preserved at all. A general watercolor effect of commercial painting systems can generate similar images.

Overall impression: All images are good in the sense that they resemble real paintings, but they are not of the quality of professionally painted ones.

7   Conclusion

Grounded in the belief that painters change their painting parameters based on their scenes and subjects, we proposed a painterly image generation method that involves searching for images with similar scenes and transferring the color and brushwork from the painting to the target picture in order to reflect the specific painter's style. We also showed through subjective evaluation experiments that the method can successfully generate a painterly image that reflects the specific painter's style. The spread and popularity of mobile devices with high-performance cameras has allowed people to photograph and capture striking scenes quickly and easily, regardless of the person's artistic ability. The Internet, meanwhile, has given people direct access to a wealth of painterly images and artistic work in a diverse array of styles. Content prosumers should thus benefit greatly from the method proposed in this paper, which makes use of pictures and Internet-based resources. Although the method works with essentially any type of painting material or painting style, the experiments in this paper used only landscape paintings by several prominent artists for copyright-related reasons. Moving forward, we plan to experiment with paintings of different subjects and styles.

Oliva and Torralba [15] have already proven that GIST feature vector, calculated by dividing an image into a grid of regions, is an effective means of ascertaining the broad, general composition of an image. By complementing GIST with the rule of thirds, we have successfully improved the accuracy of searches for similar scenes.

We now plan to develop a method that will break an image into regions based on features like color, texture, and frequency and then perform matching on the various regions. Given that painters use rough strokes and fine strokes to give their scenes basic outlines and depict the smaller details of their subjects, there is also the potential to devise a method for transferring styles to a given picture by region. It may be possible to appropriate the background and basic outlines of the painting with the most similar scene and then, instead of using the same base painting for the remaining aspects of the image, pick and choose from a selection of all the available painting samples to find the paintings that most closely match the individual regions. Deep neural network is another promising tool for painting style transferring [4]. Further improvement can be expected by combining our scene aware approach with newest deep neural network such as CNN.

The spread and popularity of mobile devices with high-performance cameras has allowed people to photograph and capture striking scenes quickly and easily, regardless of the person's artistic ability. The Internet, meanwhile, has given people direct access to a wealth of painterly images and artistic work in a diverse array of styles. Content prosumers should thus benefit greatly from the method proposed in this paper, which makes use of pictures and Internet-based resources. Although the method works with essentially any type of painting material or painting style, the experiments in this paper used only landscape paintings by several prominent artists for copyright-related reasons. Moving forward, we plan to experiment with paintings of different subjects and styles.

Acknowledgement. This work was partially supported by JSPS KAKENHI (JP16K12459, JP26560006, JP25280037).

References

1. Ashikhmin, M.: Fast texture transfer. IEEE Comput. Graph. Appl. **23**(4), 38–43 (2003)
2. Chang, C., Peng, Y., Chen, Y., Wang, S.: Artistic painting style transformation using a patch-based sampling method. J. Inform. Sci. Eng. **26**(4), 1443–1458 (2010)
3. Chang, W.H., Cheng, M.C., Kuo, C.M., Huang, G.D.: Feature-oriented artistic styles transfer based on effective texture synthesis. J. Inform. Hiding Multimedia Sig. Process. **6**(1), 29–46 (2015)
4. Gatys, L.A., Ecker, A.S., Bethge, M.: A neural algorithm of artistic style. arXiv preprint arXiv:1508.06576 (2015)
5. Guo, Y., Yu, J., Xu, X., Wang, J., Peng, Q.: Example based painting generation. J. Zhejiang Univ. Sci. A **7**(7), 1152–1159 (2006)
6. Hays, J., Efros, A.A.: Scene completion using millions of photographs. ACM Trans. Graph. **26**(3), Article 4 (2007)
7. Hegde, S., Gatzidis, C., Tian, F.: Painterly rendering techniques: a state-of-the-art review of current approaches. Comput. Animation Virtual Worlds **24**(1), 43–64 (2013)
8. Hertzmann, A., Jacobs, C., Oliver, N., Curless, B., Salesin, D.: Image analogies. In: Proceedings of SIGGRAPH, pp. 327–340 (2001)
9. Kyprianidis, J.E., Collomosse, J., Wang, T., Isenberg, T.: State of the "art": a taxonomy of artistic stylization techniques for images and video. IEEE Trans. Vis. Comput. Graph. **19**(5), 866–885 (2013)

10. Lee, H., Seo, S., Ryoo, S., Yoon, K.: Directional texture transfer. In: Proceedings of International Symposium on Non-Photorealistic Animation and Rendering, pp. 43–48 (2010)
11. Lee, H., Seo, S., Yoon, K.: Directional texture transfer with edge enhancement. Comput. Graph. **35**(1), 81–91 (2011)
12. Lee, T.Y., Yan, C.R.: Feature-based texture synthesis. In: Proceedings of International Conference on Computational Science and its Applications (2005)
13. Liu, L.G., Chen, R.J., Wolf, L., Cohen-Or, D.: Optimizing photo composition. EUROGRAPHICS **29**(2), 469–478 (2010)
14. Liu, Y., Cohen, M., Uyttendaele, M., Rusinkiewicz, S.: Autostyle: automatic style transfer from image collections to users' images. In: Computer Graphics Forum, vol. 33, pp. 21–31. Wiley Online Library (2014)
15. Oliva, A., Torralba, A.: Building the gist of a scene: the role of global image features in recognition. Vis. Percept. Prog. Brain Res. **155**, 23–36 (2006)
16. Shih, Y., Paris, S., Barnes, C., Freeman, W.T., Durand, F.: Style transfer for headshot portraits. ACM Trans. Graph. **33**(4) (2014). Article 148
17. Wang, W., Yang, H., Sun, J.: Efficient example-based painting and synthesis of 2d directional texture. IEEE Trans. Vis. Comput. Graph. **10**(3), 266–277 (2004)
18. Xie, X., Tian, F., Seah, H.S.: Feature guided texture synthesis (fgts) for artistic style transfer. In: Proceedings of International Conference on Digital Interactive Media in Entertainment and Arts, pp. 44–49 (2007)
19. Xie, X., Tian, F., Seah, H.S.: Style learning with feature-based texture synthesis. Comput. Entertainment (CIE) **6**(4), Article 25 (2008)

Privacy-Preserved Spatial Skyline Queries in Location-Based Services

Rong Tan[(⊠)] and Wen Si

Department of Information and Computer Science,
Shanghai Business School, Shanghai, China
tanrong529@gmail.com, cs6401outlook@yeah.net

Abstract. Skyline query has been investigated extensively in many fields recently. One of the interesting ones is the spatial skyline query that retrieves those points of P not dominated by any other point in P with respect to their derived spatial attributes. However, being point-based, this kind of query method is not suitable for privacy protection. In this paper, we introduce the privacy-preserved spatial skyline query where the distances calculated between the query points and the objects change from 'point to point' to 'region to point'. It is the first effort to process relative skyline queries based on a 'region to point' way. Accordingly, we proposed three approaches: BC, VRS^2 and $NVRS^2$. While BC is a straightforward method, VRS^2 and $NVRS^2$ manipulate the properties of Voronoi diagram and Network Voronoi diagram for the Euclidean space and road networks situations respectively. Furthermore, with respect to the changes of query conditions, another two algorithms DPJA and DPDA to dynamically update the results are proposed so that the heavy re-calculation could be avoided. Our empirical experiments show that our approaches have good performance in retrieving the skyline points of privacy-preserved spatial skyline query.

Keywords: Privacy-preserved · Spatial skyline query · Location-based services · Voronoi diagram · Road networks · Network voronoi diagram · Dynamical query

1 Introduction

With the advancement of wireless communication technology, sensing technology and mobile computing devices, such as PDAs and smart phones, the usage of Location-based Services (LBS) has been fundamentally promoted, while a lot of applications relating to the LBS services have been developed [1]. As for the LBS services, they include identifying the location of a person, discovering the closest gas station to a driver and navigating a tourist to scenic spots. However, most of the current LBS services are designed to support individual activities, which means only one person can benefit from the services he/she uses. Moreover, there is a lack of services to support the group activities that are actually very pervasive in daily life.

Let's assume that several friends located at different places want to gather together at a restaurant for a dinner. It is expected that the restaurant should not be far from all of them. This kind of queries has attracted some attention recently in LBS (e.g., the NN

© Springer-Verlag GmbH Germany 2017
M.L. Gavrilova et al. (Eds.): Trans. on Comput. Sci. XXX, LNCS 10560, pp. 50–72, 2017.
https://doi.org/10.1007/978-3-662-56006-8_4

query, such as GNN [2] and the ANN [3]). Both the GNN and ANN queries can find the k objects according to the minimum aggregated credit, such as the minimum total distance to a group of query points. In addition, the skyline operators are studied to solve this problem, for the Euclidean space (e.g., the Spatial Skyline queries, SSQs [4]), and for road networks (e.g., the multi-source skyline query [5]). Besides providing the result set with respect to spatial attribute, both of them can be easily adjusted to make comparisons among non-spatial attributes. However, all of these solutions have no consideration about the inquirers' privacy. It is because the locations of the query points are not perturbed, but represented as exact longitude and latitude coordinate pairs which may expose the sensitive information to the adversaries.

The privacy issues have gained huge concerns in LBS for years. The features of location awareness and ubiquitous usage of mobile devices make the privacy situations become more unimaginably complex. One efficient way to reduce location privacy risks is to promote location k-anonymity [6]. A subject is considered k-anonymous with respect to location information if and only if the location information sent from an inquirer to the location anonymizer is indistinguishable from at least $k - 1$ other subjects. If the location information sent by each query point is perturbed by replacing the exact longitude and latitude coordinate pair with a coarser grained spatial range (usually a rectangle area), such that there are $k - 1$ other query points within that range, the adversary will face the uncertainty in matching the inquirer with a location-identity association. As a result, the NN query problem will become more challenging when the distances calculated between the query points and the query objects change from 'point to point' to 'region to point'.

In this paper, we first define the privacy-preserved spatial skyline query which extends the spatial skyline query from point-based to range-based domain. Next, the corresponding dominance relation check methods are provides as well. We propose three approaches: Bisector and Candidate dominating range algorithm, Voronoi-based Range Spatial Skyline query algorithm, and Network Voronoi-based Range Spatial Skyline query algorithm, termed BC, VRS^2 and $NVRS^2$ for short. BC is a straight-forward method to retrieve the skyline points. VRS^2 is designed for Euclidean space which manipulates the properties of Voronoi diagram. Several related theorems, which can help to efficiently reduce the search space, are introduced and proved. On the other hand, with respect to the road networks situation, the Network Voronoi diagram is utilized by $NVRS^2$. It contains three phases: pre-calculation, filtering and refinement. In pre-calculation phase, the Network Voronoi diagram is pre-calculated and the related component information such as Voronoi neighbors and distance between generators and border points, etc. are all stored as well. In the filtering phase, objects are filtered if they are spatially dominated by the skyline points such as the NN points of those anonymous query areas. Thus, the searching space is reduced. In the final phase, the objects in the candidate set are refined by dominance check iteratively to retrieve the result set. Furthermore, comprehensive study has been conducted on the dynamism when the query conditions are changed. Consequently, we propose another two algorithms according to the increase and decrease situations of the data objects, so as to avoid unnecessary re-calculation and thus efficiently perform the update.

The paper is structured as follows: Sect. 2 surveys the related work; Sect. 3 introduces the definition of privacy-preserved spatial skyline query; Sect. 4 proposes the approaches BC and VRS^2 as well as two dynamic algorithms DPJA and DPDA which are all for the Euclidean space; Sect. 5 provides the NVRS^2 with respect to the road networks situation; Sect. 6 evaluates our approaches in term of the performance and dominance check, and finally, Sect. 7 concludes the paper.

2 Related Work

The NN query problem is similar to the multi-object rendezvous problem in the areas of astronautic, aeronautic and robot research communities from the geometric perspective, such as the circumcenter algorithm introduced by Ando et al. [7]. They both aim to retrieve a convergence place for multi-object. However, the algorithms proposed in these areas mostly intend to reduce the time complexity and improve the control strategies in decision support, robot control and control design issues, etc. [8]. Furthermore, they focus only on the objects, while both the inquirers and query objects shall be considered.

In the spatial databases area, several R-tree based algorithms are proposed to progressively search for the GNN [2] results in the ascending order of the aggregated credit. Papadias et al. [3] proposed algorithms for Aggregate Nearest Neighbor (ANN) queries. It can find the point with minimum aggregate distance from the query points. By minimizing the I/O and computational cost, the methods proposed there utilize R-trees and distance bounds to converge to the result. Yui [4] as well as Sun et al. [9] extended the ANN from Euclidean distance to the road networks. Zhang et al. [10] investigated the ANN query in uncertain graphs and Haitao Wang proposed the Aggregate-MAX Top-k NN searching algorithm [11]. Zhang et al. [19] focus on solving the GNN problem from the managers' perspective, and proposed the reverse top-k group nearest neighbor (RkGNN) query.

On the other hand, the Spatial Skyline Queries (SSQ) provided another way to find the potential convergence places. Given a set of data objects and a set of query points, a SSQ retrieves those points of which are not dominated by any other points in, considering their derived spatial attributes. The main difference with the general skyline query is that this spatial domination depends on the location of the query points. Two algorithms, the branch-and bound skyline algorithm (BBS) based and the Voronoi-based, as well as an algorithm has been proposed for the static query and continuous query respectively.

A range-based query can help protect the inquirer's privacy since the adversary cannot determine where the inquirer is inside the coarser grained spatial range. Hu and Lee [12] introduced the range nearest neighbor (RNN) query, after which they proposed efficient in-memory processing and secondary memory pruning techniques for RNN queries in both 2D and high-dimensional spaces. And Bao et al. [13] extended the RNN query to k-RNN query under the road networks. Hashem et al. [18] proposed a framework for privacy preserving GNN queries and introduced an efficient algorithm to evaluate GNN queries with respect to the provided set of regions.

While our work is based on the previous studies, such as the SSQs, it distinguishes itself by extending the spatial skyline query from point-based to range-based domain. It has to face more challenges, since the distance between a rectangle area and a point is not a certain value in either the Euclidean space or the road networks.

3 Problem Definition

In this section, we will define the privacy-preserved spatial skyline query which the locations of query points are perturbed by replacing the longitude and latitude coordinate pairs with rectangle areas.

Assuming the anonymous set published by the location anonymizer is represented as a rectangle (usually a minimum bounding box, MBR) in spatial space, the probability $P(q)$ of query point in any position inside this rectangle is the same. All of the rectangles covering the query points are denoted as the set Ω, and the $Dist(p, \Omega_i)$ indicates the distance between an object p and a query rectangle $\Omega_i \in \Omega$. The distance here is not specified which means it both for the Euclidean space and the road networks. In the later section, we will discuss them in details.

Definition 1. Let the set P contain the data objects in the d-dimensional space $\mathbb{R}^d$, given a set of query areas $\Omega = \{\Omega_1, \ldots, \Omega_n\}$, and the two objects p and p', and p *range spatially dominates* p' with respect to Ω, we have $Dist(p, \Omega_i) \leq Dist(p', \Omega_i)$ for all $\Omega_i \in \Omega$, and $Dist(p, \Omega_i) < Dist(p', \Omega_i)$ for some $\Omega_j \in \Omega$.

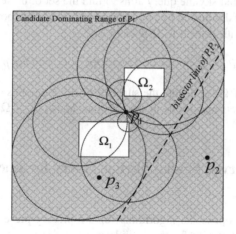

Fig. 1. The privacy-preserved spatial skyline query of three objects and two query areas.

Figure 1 shows the dominance relations of spatial skyline query among the three objects p_1, p_2 and p_3, and two query rectangle areas Ω_1 and Ω_2. For the Euclidean space, the point p_1 spatially dominates p_2 as both Ω_1 and Ω_2 are closer to p_1 than p_2. Note that if we draw the perpendicular bisector line of the line segment p_1p_2, p_1, Ω_1 and Ω_2 will be located on the same side of the bisector line while p_2 is not. Therefore, this is a useful way to check the dominance relation between two objects. Assuming two data objects p_1 and p_2 which their perpendicular bisector line divides the spatial space into two parts, p_1 range spatially dominates p_2 if p_1 and all the rectangle areas $\Omega_i \in \Omega$ are on the same side.

On the other hand, as the query point may locate at any position inside the rectangle area Ω_i, the $Dist(p, \Omega_i)$ is obviously not a certain value but ranges from the $MinDist(p, \Omega_i)$ to the $MaxDist(p, \Omega_i)$ (the $MinDist(p, \Omega_i)$ denotes the distance between the closest point inside Ω_i to p while the $MaxDist(p, \Omega_i)$ denotes the furthest). As a result, the dominance relation between p_1 and p_3 cannot be decided since the $Dist(p_1, \Omega_1)$ and $Dist(p_3, \Omega_1)$ cannot be compared (See Fig. 1).

Assuming that Ω_i is a query rectangle area and p_j is a data object, $C(p_j, \Omega_i)$ is a circle which centered at the one point on the Ω_1 with radius $Dist(\Omega_i, p_j)$. As the points are infinite, $C(p_j, \Omega_i)$ are numerous and we denote the $C(p_j, \Omega)$ as the set of all the $C(p_j, \Omega_i)$. Note that $C(p_j, \Omega)$ is the spatially dominating region of p_j. If another data object p_k locates inside the set $C(p_j, \Omega)$, thus p_j cannot range spatially dominates p_k, since p_k is possibly closer to the query point inside some Ω_i than p_j. The set $C(p_j, \Omega)$ can form a minimum bounding box, which is called the *Candidate Dominating Range*, denoted as $CDR(p)$. Any objects locate outside the $CDR(p)$ are obviously range spatially dominated by p while the objects locate inside the $CDR(p)$ may have to be checked of the correct dominance relation (e.g., although p_2 is inside $CDR(p_1)$, it is range spatially dominated by p_1, see Fig. 1). Here, the intersections of all the $CDR(p)$ are referred as the *Candidate Region* (*CR*) where all the skyline points are inside it.

Definition 2. Given the set P of data objects and the set Ω of query rectangle areas, the privacy-preserved spatial skyline query aims to find the set of those objects in P which are not range spatially dominated by any other objects in P. The point p is in the range spatial skyline of P with respect to Ω if there is:

$$\forall p' \in P, p' \neq p, \exists \Omega_i \in \Omega \ s.t. \ Dist(p, \Omega_i) \leq Dist(p', \Omega_i)$$

Finally, we use $SS(\Omega)$ to denote the superset of skyline points of P with respect to Ω, since the query points may locate at any positions inside $\Omega_i \in \Omega$, thus leading to the result of a superset.

4 Privacy-Preserved Spatial Skyline Query for Euclidean Space

In this section, we propose the algorithms for the privacy-preserved spatial skyline query with different strategies for the Euclidean space.

4.1   Bisector and Candidate Dominating Range Algorithm (BC)

The basic idea of this algorithm is to combine the methods of perpendicular bisector line and the candidate dominating range to find the skyline points. As demonstrated in Fig. 1, although the set $C(p_1, \Omega)$ could be used to determine the spatial dominance relationship between p_1 and p_2 as well as p_1 and p_3, it could cost a lot. Consequently, the perpendicular bisector line can help to check dominance relations so as to reduce the total computation.

Theorem 1. Given two data objects p and p', and their perpendicular bisector line divides the space into two parts, namely S_p and $S_{p'}$. If for any query area $\Omega_i \in \Omega$, there is $\Omega_i \in S_p$, and then, p spatially dominates p'.

Proof. Making the perpendicular bisector line of p and p', it divides the space into S_p and $S_{p'}$. Obviously, for any point p_i in S_p, there is $Dist(p, p_i) \leq Dist(p', p_i)$. Therefore, if all $\Omega_i \in \Omega$ locates inside S_p, then p spatially controls p'.

Theorem 2. For any $\Omega_i \in \Omega$, the data object p which is closest to it belongs to $SS(\Omega)$.

Proof. Each object p can be represented as an n-dimensional point where the ith attributes is the distance from p to Ω_i. If p is the closest point to Ω_i, then at least with respect to the ith attribute, it would not be controlled by any other objects, thereby proving that $p \in SS(\Omega)$.

We denote the $NN(\Omega_i)$ to represent the closest object to the query area Ω_i in the following paper.

BC algorithm is a straightforward algorithm for privacy-preserved spatial skyline query. There are two phases in this algorithm. In the first phase, it starts with finding one of the $NN(\Omega_i)$ such as p by R-tree index to be the first skyline point belongs to the $SS(\Omega)$. Then its candidate dominating range $CDR(p)$ is computed, any other data objects which are not inside the $CDR(p)$ will be filtered. Objects which are not controlled by p will be joined into a candidate set. This phase is able to reduce the search space.

In the second phase, the potential skyline points in the candidate set will be checked in pairs following the Theorem 1 iteratively. After all the potential data objects in candidate set are visited, the final result set $SS(\Omega)$ can be obtained.

4.2   Voronoi-Based Range Spatial Skyline Query Algorithm (VRS²)

BC algorithm provides a method to reduce the search space and to retrieve the skyline points of privacy-preserved spatial skyline query. However, its efficiency is not satisfied. In order to solve this problem, another algorithm which is mainly based on the Voronoi diagram and the convex hull is proposed. We call it the *Voronoi-based Range Spatial Skyline Query Algorithm, VRS²*. Before we introduce how the VRS² algorithm works in details, some important definitions and theorems would be proposed and proved first.

Convex hull and Voronoi diagram are two important knowledge aspects relating to computational geometry [14]. The convex hull means a minimum convex polygon, concerning which all points will be on the polygon edge or within. And it can be formally defined as:

Definition 3. A set is *convex* if for any two points $p, q \in S$, the line segment $pq \subset S$. And given a finite set of points $P = \{p_1, \ldots, p_n\}$, the *convex hull* of P is the smallest convex set C such that $P \subset C$.

The Voronoi polygon and Voronoi diagram can be formally defined as:

Definition 4. Assuming a set of generators $P = \{p_1, \ldots, p_n\}$, the region given by:

$$VP(p_i) = \{p | d(p, p_i) \leq d(p, p_j)\} \, for \, j \neq i$$

where $d(p, p_i)$ specifies the minimum distance between p and p_i in Euclidean space is called the *Voronoi Polygon* associated with p_i, and the set given by:

$$VD(P) = \{VP(p_1), \ldots, VP(p_n)\}$$

is called the Voronoi Diagram generated by P.

Theorem 3. For any $\Omega_i \in \Omega$, the data object p which is closest to it must be the generator point p whose $VP(p)$ the Ω_i locates inside or intersects with.

Proof. According to the Definition 4, the Theorem 3 is easily proved.

Theorem 4. For the rectangle query area set Ω, if their convex hull is represented as $CH(\Omega)$. Then, for any object p which locates inside $CH(\Omega)$, it belongs to $SS(\Omega)$.

Proof. The proof by contrapositive is used. Assume that p does not belong to $SS(\Omega)$, then there is one object p' which spatially range dominate p. According to Theorem 1, if drawing the perpendicular bisector line of segment pp', all the query areas $\Omega_i \in \Omega$ will be located in the divided space $S_{p'}$. Therefore, $CH(\Omega)$ should locate in $S_{p'}$ as well which makes the conflict with the known condition that p locates inside $CH(\Omega)$. Thus, the theorem is proved.

Theorem 5. If data object p whose Voronoi polygon $VP(p)$ intersects with the convex hull $CH(\Omega)$, then $p \in SS(\Omega)$.

Proof. The proof by contrapositive is used. Suppose $p \notin SS(\Omega)$, and there is certainly one object p' spatially control p. Ibid seen, $VP(p)$ as well as the intersection of $VP(p)$ and $CH(\Omega)$ will locate on the same side of p'. However, it can be seen from the Definition 4. that $VP(p)$ cannot be at the side of p', so it is a contradiction. Thus, the theorem is proved.

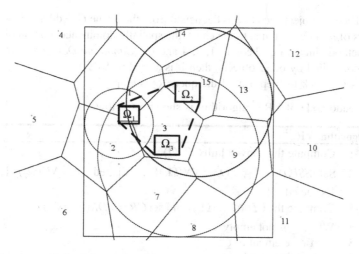

Fig. 2. The convex hull of three rectangle query areas and the voronoi diagram generated by fifteen data objects.

The VRS^2 algorithm is mainly based on above theorems. The intuition is that the VPs can be directly used to find the NN object of a query area by utilizing an index structure. As a result, the first skyline point can be retrieved in a very short time. Subsequently, in addition to filtering the searching space, based on the properties of Voronoi diagram, its adjacency information can be utilized to provide a candidate set for other skyline points. Finally, the refine process in VRS^2 is to iteratively check the spatial dominance relation in the candidate set and retrieve the result set $SS(\Omega)$.

The VRS^2 works by the following six steps:

Step 1 - The Voronoi diagram is pre-calculated, and its corresponding VPs and adjacent information are stored in a table.

Step 2 - The convex hull which covers all the privacy-preserved query area set Ω is calculated and to utilize the index structure such as R-tree to the find one of the $NN(\Omega_i)$.

Step 3 - The Voronoi neighbors of $NN(\Omega_i)$ are put into a queue Q.

Step 4 - Two lists namely the visited list and extracted list are maintained to track the traversal process. The visited list contains all the visited objects, and the extracted list contains the objects whose Vornoi neighbors have been visited.

Step 5 - The first object such as q is dequeued from the queue Q. Add all of the Vornoi neighbors of q to Q. And then to the check the spatially dominance relation of q based on the methods including Theorem 1, 3, 4 and the *Candidate Dominance Region*. If q is not controlled by other objects, then it is stored in $SS(\Omega)$.

Step 6 - Go back to Step 5 until the queue Q is empty.

The pseudo-code of VRS^2 algorithm is shown as below.

Algorithm VRS^2

1	Compute the convex hull $CH(\Omega)$;
2	Set $SS(\Omega)=\{\}$, $Q=\{NN(\Omega_1)\}$, Visited $=\{\ NN(\Omega_i)\ \}$, Extracted$=\{\}$
3	Compute the $CDR(NN(\Omega_1))$ and set $CR=CDR(NN(\Omega_1))$;
4	While Q is not empty
5	q=first element of Q;
6	if $q \in$ Extracted
7	remove q from Q;
8	if q is inside $CH(\Omega)$
	or $VP(q)$ intersects with $CH(\Omega)$
	or q is not dominated by $SS(\Omega)$
9	add q to $SS(\Omega)$;
10	if q dominate any object inside $SS(\Omega)$ such as q'
11	remove q' from $SS(\Omega)$;
12	set $CR=CR \cap CDR(q)$;
13	else
14	add q to Extracted;
15	if $SS(\Omega)=\varnothing$ or a Voronoi neighbor of q is in $SS(\Omega)$
16	for each Voronoi neighbor of q such as q'
17	if $q' \in$ Visited, discard q';
18	if q' is inside CR
19	add q' to Visited;
20	add q' to Q;
21	Return $SS(\Omega)$;

Here, we explain the specific process of VRS2 algorithm based on the example shown in Fig. 2. There are three rectangle query areas Ω_1, Ω_2 and Ω_3, and fifteen data objects by which the Voronoi diagram is generated. The convex hull $CH(\Omega)$ is first computed, as indicated by a thick dashed line. Then, three arrays including $SS(\Omega)$, visited list and extracted list have been initialized. Put the nearest point $NN(\Omega_1)$ with respect to Ω_1 an empty queue Q and calculate its area $CDR(p_1)$ as the initial candidate region set CR which is indicated by the thin solid rectangle in Fig. 2. Subsequently, all the Vornoi neighbors of p_1 will be checked in turn. If the object is in CR, it will be put into the queue Q and will be recorded in the visited list as well. As in Fig. 2, the objects p_2, p_3, p_{14} and p_{15} are joined into the queue Q, but p_4 and p_5 will not because they are not inside CR. Then, p_1 is removed from the queue Q, and put into the result set $SS(\Omega)$. Algorithm then dequeues p_2 from the queue Q, and checks all its Vornoi neighbors as the same process of p_1. Subsequently, p_2 is recorded into the extracted list. The spatial dominance relation is checked. Since the Voronoi Polygon $VP(p_2)$ intersects with the convex hull, p_2 belongs to $SS(\Omega)$ according to the Theorem 4. Finally, to make the intersection of $CDR(p_2)$ with the original CR to form the new CR. After processing all the objects in the queue, the final skyline set $SS(\Omega)$ will be obtained.

Table 1 describes the change of the elements in queue Q and the result set $SS(\Omega)$ of VRS^2 algorithm of the example in Fig. 2. The result of the privacy-preserved spatial skyline query contains p_1, p_2, p_3 and p_{15}. And the inquirers can further make their choice according to other conditions such as price, quality of services and so on.

Table 1. The change of Q and $SS(\Omega)$.

Steps	Objects in Q	$SS(\Omega)$
1	p_1	$\varnothing$
2	$p_1, p_2, p_3, p_{14}, p_{15},$	$\varnothing$
4	$p_2, p_3, p_{14}, p_{15}, p_7$	p_1
6	$p_3, p_{14}, p_{15}, p_7, p_8, p_9$	p_1, p_2
...	...	p_1, p_2, p_3, p_{15}

4.3 Approaches for Dynamic Query Conditions

In the practical queries, the inquirers always adjust their query conditions, for which the queried objects would change accordingly. If every change of the query condition takes a new calculation, then there would be too much consumption. A better method is to utilize the output of the last calculation and dynamically updating the result set according to the new query condition. Without any doubt, this method could reduce the calculation consumption and acquire better performance.

Let's take the example shown in Fig. 2 for instance. We assume all queried points are restaurants belonging to different cooking styles which have been classified in Table 2. Assume that the first query condition includes all restaurants, which means the whole 15 objects. Then the result set shown as Table 2 contains p_1, p_2, p_3 and p_{15}. If the inquirers change their query condition, and they want to find all the Chinese restaurants, then $p_3, p_4, p_6, p_8, p_{10}$ and p_{12} would be all deleted from the data object set, while only the remaining objects need to calculated. During the first query, p_3 spatially controls the points p_7 and p_9, so these two points cannot be in the result set $SS(\Omega)$. Now in the second query, due to the change of the query condition, p_3 is no longer the queried object. As a result, p_7 and p_9 have not be controlled by any other objects. Hence, the new query result $SS(\Omega)$ should be changed to p_1, p_2, p_7, p_9 and p_{15}.

Table 2. Classification of the data objects.

No	Objects	Styles
1	$p_1, p_2, p_5, p_7, p_9, p_{11}, p_{13}, p_{14}, p_{15}$	Chinese cuisine
2	p_3, p_8, p_{10}	Western cuisine
3	p_4, p_6, p_{12}	Japanese cuisine

Therefore, under the new query condition, if the queried data object is removed which results in the decrease of the original result set, then the impact incurred by the removed object should be recalculated instead of conducting a new complete calculation. Similarly, if a new queried data object is joined, the new result can be achieved by checking the dominance relations in pair between the new object with skyline points in the original result set. Below, we will introduce two dynamic update algorithms with respect to the new query conditions of decrease and increase of data objects respectively.

4.3.1   Dynamic Point Joining Algorithm (DPJA)

In case of a new data object being queried, if the new object locates outside the candidate region CR formed by the original skyline points, it does not affect the original result set. It is because at this time the new data object will certainly be spatially controlled by a skyline point in $SS(\Omega)$. Furthermore, when the new data object is inside CR, it may have an impact on the original result set which we should to check.

In Fig. 3, for example, the new joined data object is p', and its candidate dominating region is CDR(p') which can be used to intersect with the original candidate region CR to construct the new CR (shaded rectangle in Fig. 4). At this time, if there is skyline point in original result set which is outside the new CR (which is in the area indicated by the symbol of "−"). It shall be removed from the result set since it has been controlled by the p'. In terms of the new CR, it will also need to conduct the dominance check in pairs with p'. In this way, the updated result set can be obtained. We call this method the Dynamic Point Joining Algorithm (DPJA).

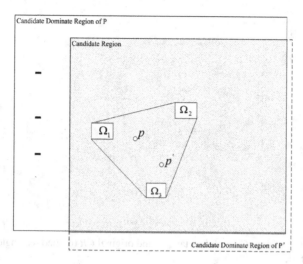

Fig. 3. New *CR* (shaded rectangle) formed after the new object joined.

The pseudo-code of DPJA is shown as below:

Algorithm DPJA
---
01 set $SS(\Omega)' = SS(\Omega)$;

02 for each adding point such as p'

03   if p' is outside the *CR*

04   return $SS(\Omega)'$;

05   else

06   compute the $CDR(p')$;

07   if $CR \cap CDR(p') \neq CR$

08   set $CR = CR \cap CDR(p')$;

09   for each $p_i \in SS(\Omega)$ such as p

10   if p is not inside the *CR*

11   or p is dominated by p'

12   delete p from $SS(\Omega)'$

13   else

14   return $SS(\Omega)'$;

15   return $SS(\Omega)'$;

4.3.2   Dynamic Point Deleting Algorithm (DPDA)

If the reduced data object is not the skyline point in the original result, then the new query results are the same as the original one. On the contrary, the new query condition may lead to a new result set.

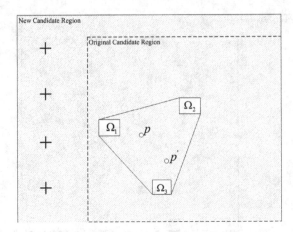

Fig. 4. Comparison of new *CR* (solid rectangle) and original *CR* (dashed rectangle) with respect to the removal of p'.

In Fig. 4, when the skyline point p' is deleted, new *CR* has changed from the dashed rectangle to solid rectangle which result in that the objects locate inside the area indicated by "+" may belong to the new result set. Our approach first calculates the new *CR* formed by the remaining skyline points, and then compare with the original *CR* to obtain the difference area. If other objects are inside this region, then dominance control check will be conducted. If they are not controlled, then they would be added to the new result set. We call it the *Dynamic Point Deleting Algorithm* (DPDA). Its pseudo-code is as follows:

Algorithm DPDA
---
01 set $SS(\Omega)' = SS(\Omega)$;
02 for each deleting point such as p'
03   if p' is outside the CR
04   return $SS(\Omega)'$;
05   else
06   set $CR' = CDR(p_i)$; $p_i \in SS(\Omega)$
07   for each rest $p_j \in SS(\Omega)$ such as p
08   compute the $CDR(p)$;
09   set $CR' = CR' \cap CDR(p)$;
10   set $R = CR' - CR$;
11   if $R > 0$
12   for each point inside R such as p''
13   if p'' is not dominated by $SS(\Omega)'$
14   add p'' to $SS(\Omega)'$;
15   return $SS(\Omega)'$;
---

5 Privacy-Preserved Spatial Skyline Query in Road Networks

Both BC and VRS^2 are based on the Euclidean space. However, in the environment with spatial network databases (SNDB), objects are restricted to move on pre-defined paths (e.g., roads). It means that the shortest distances between objects (e.g., the vehicle and the restaurants) depend on the connectivity of the network rather than their locations. As a result, while the main jobs of both BC and VRS^2 are to reduce number of data objects to be checked, the network based algorithm has to face the challenge of network distance calculation. For the privacy-preserved spatial skyline query in road networks, we proposed a Network Voronoi-based Range Spatial Skyline Query Algorithm, namely NVRS^2.

Besides the distance calculation, with the SNDB, the anonymous set published by the location anonymizer is much different in road networks. It may include both the user set and the road segments set. Unlike the BC and VRS^2, query objects are supposed to locate at any position on the road segments in NVRS^2. Therefore, the spatial dominating relation check is much more complicated in road networks than in the Euclidean space.

5.1 Anonymous Set and Network Voronoi Diagram

For the Euclidean space, since the anonymous set is only related to the locations of users. It is easily to use a minimum bounding box (e.g., usually a rectangle) spatially covering certain number (e.g., k users) of users' locations to protect the privacy. However, in road networks, the anonymous set is requested to contain both the set of users and the set of road segments. In this paper, the anonymous set in road networks is defined as follows:

Definition 5. Assuming a set of users S_u and a set of road segments S_r, if both S_u and S_r satisfy the following conditions:

1. $|S_u| \geq K$, where $|S_u|$ is the number of users;
2. $|S_r| \geq L$, where $|S_r|$ is the number of road segments;
3. $\forall u \in S_u, \exists e \in S_r, u \in e$, where $u \in e$ means that u is located on the edge e;

then set of users S_u is satisfied with the (K, L)-privacy model. If the query object $p \in S_u$ is protected by the (K, L)-privacy model, we denote $\Omega_p(K, L)$ to be the rectangle area which spatially covers the road segments set S_r.

Note that, since the spatial dominating relation check is shifted from Euclidean distance to network distance, the border points of road segments on the edges of $\Omega_p(K, L)$ play more important roles in distance calculation instead of the four vertexes of $\Omega_p(K, L)$.

On the other hand, a network Voronoi diagram (termed *NVD*) is a specialization of a Voronoi diagram in which the locations of objects are restricted to the network edges and the distance between objects is defined as the length of the shortest network distance (e.g., shortest path), instead of the Euclidean distance.

Definition 6. Given a weighted graph $G(N, E)$ consisting of a set of nodes $N = \{p_1, \ldots p_n, p_{n+1}, \ldots p_o\}$, where the first n elements are the Voronoi generators and a set of edges $E = \{e_1, \ldots, e_k\}$ which connects the nodes. The shortest network distance between an object p to p_i is defined as $d_n(p, p_i)$, then set *dominance region* and *border points* are define as follows:

$$Dom(p_i, p_j) = \{p | p \overset{k}{\underset{o=1}{\cup}} e_o, \ d_n(p, p_i) \leq d_n(p, p_j), \ i \neq j\}$$

$$b(p_i, p_j) = \{p | p \overset{k}{\underset{o=1}{\cup}} e_o, \ d_n(p, p_i) = d_n(p, p_j), \ i \neq j\}$$

$Dom(p_i, p_j)$ is called the dominance region of p_i over p_j in E which means all points in all edges that closer to p_i than p_j. And the $b(p_i, p_j)$ represents all points in all edges in E that are equally distanced from p_i to p_j.

Consequently, the Voronoi edge set related to p_i and *network Voronoi diagram* are defined as following, respectively:

$$V_{edge}(p_i) = \underset{j \in I_n \setminus \{i\}}{\cap} Dom(p_i, p_j)$$

$$NVD(P) = \{V_{edge}(p_i), \ldots, V_{edge}(p_n)\}$$

where $V_{edge}(p_i)$ represents all the points in all edges in E are closer to p_i than any other generator point in N. And the $NVP(p_i)$ represents the Network Voronoi Polygon which contains the generator point p_i. More specifically, the elements of NVD are mutually exclusive and collectively exhaustive.

5.2 Network Voronoi-Based Range Spatial Skyline Query Algorithm, NVRS^2

NVRS^2 is based on the properties of the Network Voronoi diagram. In particular, the theorems proved in the Subsect. 4.2 are still applicable to NVRS^2 when changing the Voronoi diagram to Network Voronoi diagram. However, when calculating the $CDR(p)$ of object p and checking the spatial dominance relations, the methods of VRS^2 are no longer useful.

For example, Fig. 5 depicts a privacy-preserved spatial skyline query in road networks. The Network Voronoi diagram is generated by the three object point p_1, p_2 and p_3. The numbers on each edge stand for the edge weights (e.g., distance), and the set of $I = \{I_1, \ldots, I_{13}\}$ represents the intersection nodes of road networks. The set of border points $B = \{b_1, \ldots, b_7\}$ along with the point v construct the border edges of $NVP(p_1)$, $NVP(p_2)$ and $NVP(p_3)$. The query object q_1 and q_2 locate on one of the road segments inside the two privacy-preserved query regions $\Omega_{q_1}(3, 2)$ and $\Omega_{q_2}(3, 2)$ which satisfy the $(3, 2)$-privacy model. The other query objects used to help construct the anonymous set are not marked since it is not necessary here. The query regions Ω_{q_1} and Ω_{q_2} intersect with the road networks at the point sets $S_{\Omega_{q_1}} = \{s_1, s_2, s_3\}$ and $S_{\Omega_{q_2}} = \{s_4, s_5, s_6, s_7, s_8\}$. Note that, as the $NVP(p_1)$ and $NVP(p_3)$ intersect with the query regions Ω_{q_1} and Ω_{q_2}, according to the Theorem 4, objects p_1 and p_3 are the skyline points. However, with respect to the object p_2, although both Ω_{q_1} and Ω_{q_2} locate at the same side of the S_{p_1} divided by the perpendicular bisector line of the line segment p_1p_2, p_2 is not certainly spatially controlled by p_1 since the distance calculation is shifted to network distance instead of Euclidean distance.

For the query region Ω_{q_2}, since the location of query object q_2 may locate at any road segments inside Ω_{q_2}, the distance between object p_1 and Ω_{q_2} ranges from $min\{d_n(p_1, s_i), \ldots, d_n(p_1, s_n)\}$ to $max\{d_n(p_1, s_i), \ldots, d_n(p_1, s_n)\}$. Assume that the s_5 and s_7 are the intersection border points of Ω_{q_2} which respectively have the minimum and maximum network distance to the object p_1. Then the minimum distance from p_1 to Ω_{q_2} can be calculated as:

$$
\begin{aligned}
d_n(p_1, s_5) &= min(d_n(p_1, b_5) + d_n(b_5, s_5), \ d_n(p_1, b_7) + d_n(b_7, s_5)) \\
&= d_n(p_1, I_1) + d_n(I_1, I_7) + d_n(I_7, b_5) + d_n(b_5, s_5) \\
&= 12 + d_n(b_5, s_5)
\end{aligned}
$$

And the maximum distance from p_1 to Ω_{q_2} can be calculated as:

$$
\begin{aligned}
d_n(p_1, s_7) &= min(d_n(p_1, b_5) + d_n(b_5, s_7), \ d_n(p_1, b_7) + d_n(b_7, s_7)) \\
&= d_n(p_1, I_1) + d_n(I_1, I_7) + d_n(I_7, I_{10}) + d_n(I_{10}, s_7) \\
&= 14 + d_n(I_{10}, s_7)
\end{aligned}
$$

Similarly, for the object p_2, assume that s_7 and s_8 are the intersection border points of Ω_{q_2} which respectively have the minimum and maximum network distance to p_2. Then the minimum distance from p_2 to Ω_{q_2} can be calculated as:

$$
\begin{aligned}
d_n(p_2, s_7) &= min(d_n(p_2, b_1) + d_n(b_1, s_7), \ d_n(p_2, b_2) + d_n(b_2, s_7), \\
&\quad\ d_n(p_2, b_3) + d_n(b_3, s_7), d_n(p_2, b_4) + d_n(b_4, s_7), \\
&\quad\ d_n(p_2, b_6) + d_n(b_6, s_7)) \\
&= d_n(p_2, I_6) + d_n(I_6, I_8) + d_n(I_8, I_{10}) + d_n(I_{10}, s_7) \\
&= 13 + d_n(I_{10}, s_7)
\end{aligned}
$$

And the maximum distance from p_2 to Ω_{q_2} can be calculated as:

$$
\begin{aligned}
d_n(p_2, s_8) &= min(d_n(p_2, b_1) + d_n(b_1, s_8), \ d_n(p_2, b_2) + d_n(b_2, s_8), \\
&\quad\ d_n(p_2, b_3) + d_n(b_3, s_8), d_n(p_2, b_4) + d_n(b_4, s_8), \\
&\quad\ d_n(p_2, b_6) + d_n(b_6, s_8)) \\
&= d_n(p_2, I_6) + d_n(I_6, I_8) + d_n(I_8, I_{10}) + d_n(I_{10}, s_8) \\
&= 13 + d_n(I_{10}, s_8)
\end{aligned}
$$

The result shows that the networks distance between p_1 and Ω_{q_2} ranges from $12 + d_n(b_5, s_5)$ to $14 + d_n(I_{10}, s_7)$ while the network distance between p_2 and Ω_{q_2}

ranges from $13 + d_n(I_{10}, s_7)$ to $13 + d_n(I_{10}, s_8)$. Note that the minimum network distance between p_2 and Ω_{q_2} is $13 + d_n(I_{10}, s_7)$ which is shorter than the maximum network distance between p_1 and Ω_{q_2}. Therefore, p_1 cannot spatially dominate p_2 with respect to Ω_{q_2}.

Similarly, the calculation of CDR in road networks is quite different. For the Euclidean space, since the query object may locate at any position inside the anonymous area, the four vertexes of the anonymous rectangle and the point which has the shortest vertical distance from the object p are very important. Accordingly, the $CDR(p)$ is constructed by these points. However, in the road networks, query objects are restricted to locate at the pre-defined path. Therefore, the intersections of anonymous set are utilized to calculate the CDR instead of the vertexes etc. For instance, in Fig. 5, with respect to p_1 and Ω_{q_1}, Ω_{q_1} intersects the road networks with the set $S_{\Omega_{q_1}} = \{s_1, s_2, s_3\}$. Consequently, the $CDR(p)$ is a minimum bounding box which spatially covers three circles $C(p_1, s_1)$, $C(p_1, s_2)$ and $C(p_1, s_3)$. In particular, $C(p_i, s_j)$ represents the circle whose center is s_j and the radius is $d_n(p_i, s_j)$. As the Euclidean distance must be greater than or equal to the network distance, any data objects locate outside the $CDR(p)$ will certainly be controlled by p. Thus, the search space can be reduced.

The NVRS[2] algorithm consists of the follows phases:

1. Pre-calculation phase: The Network Voronoi diagram is pre-calculated. And its corresponding VPs as well as the adjacent information are stored in a table. In addition, the border points' information of the generator points and their network distance are calculated. These data are stored and indexed as well (See Fig. 6).
2. Filtering phase: To simultaneously find the NN object of each $\Omega_i \in \Omega$, calculate their $CDRs$ respectively, and construct the CR to filter the objects which are controlled by these NN objects. And the objects which are inside the CR are put into a candidate set. Thus, the search space is efficiently reduced.

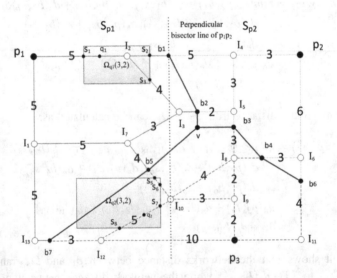

Fig. 5. An example of privacy-preserved spatial skyline query in the Network Voronoi diagram.

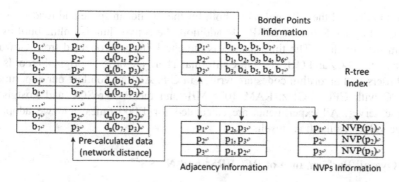

Fig. 6. The storage schema of NVRS² based on the example of Fig. 5

3. Refinement phase: All the objects in candidate set are further to be checked the dominance relations iteratively. In particular, the distance between the object p to each Ω_i ranges from $min\{d_n(p, \Omega_i)\}$ to $max\{d_n(p, \Omega_i)\}$. After the process of spatial dominance check, the skyline points are retrieved.

6 Performance Evaluation

To evaluate the performance of the algorithms proposed, we have conducted some experiments. We use three datasets in real world. The first dataset is the road network of California provided by [15]. There are 1965206 nodes and 2766607 edges, and we adopts one part of the whole network with about 20138 nodes and 21846 edges. The second dataset is POI of California [16]. There are more than 130000 pieces of data in total, and we select 10000, 20000 and 50000 according to the road networks we picked to build the Voronoi diagram and the Network Voronoi diagram by the parallel Dijkstra

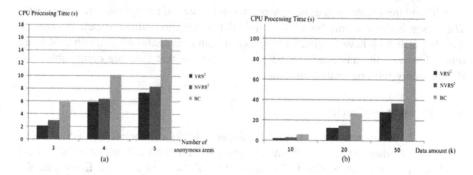

Fig. 7. Query process time of BC, VRS² and NVRS² for different number of anonymous areas and different data amount.

algorithm [17]. All the *VPs* and *NVPs* both for the Euclidean space and road networks are indexed by the R-tree on MBRs. In addition, the convex hull is online built by the Graham scan method. The third dataset is the check-in data collected from Gowalla[1] between Feb. 2009 and Oct. 2010 in California. There are 667821 original records and 15039 users. All algorithm codes are written in C #. And we conduct our experiments on a PC with CPU 2 GHz, RAM 1024 MB, and the PostgreSQL and Postgis[2] as database server. All experiments are calculated for 1,000 times, and we adopt the average values as the final results.

6.1   Overall Performance of BC, VRS^2 and $NVRS^2$

In the first experiment, we use 10000 data as the data volume to evaluate the CPU processing time, while the number of anonymous query areas is 3, 4 and 5 respectively. In particular, all the anonymous query areas satisfy with the 3-anonymity model which means each anonymous contains at least 3 users. As can be seen in Fig. 7(a), VRS^2 and $NVRS^2$ algorithms are significantly better than BC algorithm. Under the condition that the number of privacy-preserved areas is 3, 4 and 5, both VRS^2 and $NVRS^2$ take nearly half time of BC. Note that $NVRS^2$ is a little slower than VRS^2, because the shortest network distance calculated by the Dijkstra algorithm costs more time.

The second experiment evaluates the data amount effect on the processing time. The number of anonymous query areas is 3, and satisfied with the 3-anonymity model as the first experiment. We take 10000, 20000, and 50000 as the queried data objects. As shown in Fig. 7(b), we can figure that with the increase of data objects, the advantages of Voronoi-based algorithm are more obvious than the straightforward method due to the amount of spatially dominance check of VRS^2 and $NVRS^2$ are much less.

In the third experiment, the VRS^2 and $NVRS^2$ algorithms are compared with the REGION-kGNN algorithm proposed in [18] as both are aim to evaluate the GNN queries with respect to the provided set of regions (the users' imprecise locations). We also use 10000 data as the data volume to evaluate the CPU processing time, while the number of anonymous query areas is 3, 4 and 5 respectively.

We see in Fig. 8 that the time requires by REGION-kGNN is less than VRS^2 and $NVRS^2$ and the tendency is more obvious when the size of anonymous areas increases. The reason is that not only both VRS^2 and $NVRS^2$ have to online compute the convex hull, but also they have to check the spatial dominance relationship which cost more time. However, the advantage of VRS^2 or $NVRS^2$ is that they are compatible with skyline query with no-spatial attributes.

6.2   Dominance Check

Figure 8 shows the amount of spatial dominance checks conducted by VRS^2.

In Fig. 9, when the amount of data objects is 10,000, the VRS^2 only conducts about 1000 dominance check which is less than 10% of the total amount. Even with the

---

[1] http://www.gowalla.com/.

[2] http://www.postgis.org/.

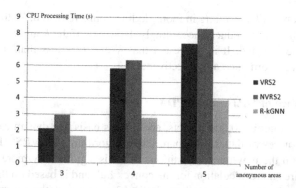

Fig. 8. Query process time of VRS^2, NVRS^2 and REGION-kGNN.

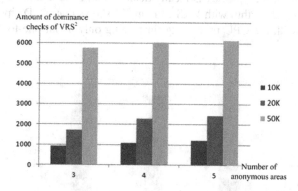

Fig. 9. Amount of spatial dominance checks conducted by VRS^2.

increase of data objects, the amount of dominance checks stabilizes below 15% of the total size. Especially, with the increase of the query areas, the amount of dominance checks does not change a lot. It shows that the dominance check is not sensitive to the number of query areas.

As for the NVRS^2, since its filtering phase is similar to VRS^2 which leads to a similar phenomenon with the same amount of objects. However, different (K, L)-model will affect the dominance checks. As shown in Table 3, it can be seen that with the increase of K and L, the amount of dominance checks decreases. It is because that with the increase of K and L, those anonymous areas have to cover more space. Then, they

Table 3. Dominance checks of NVRS^2 with different (K, L)-model

L\K	3	4	5
3	942	892	765
4	881	833	774
5	785	783	779
6	773	778	775

intersect with more *NVP*s resulting in more skyline points retrieved. With more skyline points, the search space is reduced accordingly. However, if the K and L are too big, the result will not be satisfied. It is suggested that K and L is less than 4, leading to a balance between performance and effectiveness.

6.3   Performance of DPJA and DPDA

The basic data amount is 10,000 objects, and on this basis, we dynamically add 1000, 2000 and 3000 pieces of data to compare DPJA algorithm with VRS^2. From Fig. 10, we can see that in the new query condition, DPJA is significantly more efficient than VRS^2 as it requires no recalculation for the convex hull and is based on the latest query result. It only costs about one tenth of VRS^2. Therefore, if the query condition is changed, it is wise to utilize the DPJA to get the new result instead of VRS^2.

In the final experiment, we dynamically delete 1000, 2000 and 3000 pieces of data to compare DPDA algorithm with VRS^2. Figure 11 shows that, DPDA performs better than the VRS^2, with the CPU processing time being only about one-fourth of it.

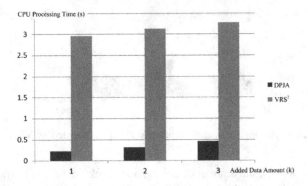

Fig. 10. DPJA v.s. VRS^2 with the added objects of 1k, 2k and 3k.

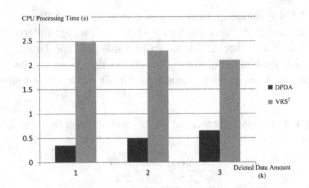

Fig. 11. DPDA v.s. VRS^2 with the deleted objects of 1k, 2k and 3k.

7 Conclusion

With popularity of wireless communications technology and the rapid development of sensor technology as well as portable computing devices, there would be great development potential for the future location-based services. Improving the efficiency of existing query algorithm, researching the new query algorithm under the new scenarios, and protecting the privacy of inquirers will be the research focuses.

This paper defines the privacy-preserved spatial skyline query issue with respect to which three novel algorithms have been proposed under the Euclidean space and road networks situations. It is the first effort to process relative skyline queries based on an 'area to point' way. Both the VRS^2 and NVRS^2 manipulate the properties of Voronoi diagram to reduce the search space and thus improve the overall performance. With respect to the dynamic query conditions, two algorithms DPJA and DPDA are developed so as to avoid the re-calculations.

Acknowledgments. This work is supported by Shanghai Natural Science Foundation (Grant No. 15ZR1430000).

References

1. Jiang, B., Yao, X.: Location based services and GIS in perspective. Environment and Urban System **30**(6), 712–725 (2006)
2. Papadias, D., Shen, Q., Tao, Y., Mouratids, K.: Group nearest neighbor queries. In: ICDE 2004 (2004)
3. Yiu, M.L., Mamoulis, N., Papadias, D.: Aggregate nearest neighbor queries in road networks. IEEE Trans. Knowl. Data Eng. **17**(6), 820–833 (2005)
4. Sharifzadeh, M., Shahabi, C.: The spatial skyline queries. In: VLDB, Seoul, pp. 751–762 (2006)
5. Deng, K., Zhou, X., Shen, H.T.: Multi-source skyline query processing in road networks. In: ICDE, pp. 796–805 (2007)
6. Gedik, B., Liu, L.: Protecting location privacy with personalized k-anonymity: architecture and algorithms. Journal of IEEE Trans. on Mobile Computing **7**(1), 1–18 (2008)
7. Ando, H., Oasa, Y., Suzuki, I., Yamashita, M.: Distributed memoryless point convergence algorithm for mobile robots with limited visibility. IEEE Trans. Robot. Autom. **15**(5), 818–828 (1999)
8. Lin, J., Morse, A.S., Anderson, B.D.O.: The multi-agent rendezvous problem. In: Proceedings of 42nd IEEE Conference on Decision and Control, New Haven, pp. 1508–1513 (2003)
9. Sun, W.W., Chen, C.N., Zhu, L., Gao, Y.J., Jing, Y.N., Li, Q.: On efficient aggregate nearest neighbor query processing in road networks. J. Comput. Sci. Technol. **30**(4), 781–798 (2015)
10. Zhang, L., Chaokun, W., Wang, J.: Aggregate nearest neighbor queries in uncertain graphs. J. World Wide Web **17**(1), 161–188 (2014)
11. Wang, H.: Aggregate-MAX top-k nearest neighbor searching in the L1 plane. Int. J. Comput. Geom. **25**, 57–76 (2015)
12. Hu, H., Lee, D.L.: Range nearest-neighbor query. IEEE Trans. Knowl. Data Eng. **18**(1), 78–91 (2006)

13. Bao, J., Chow, C.Y., Mokbel, M.F., Ku, W.S.: Efficient evaluation of k-range nearest neighbour queries in road networks. In: Proceedings of 11th International Conference on Mobile Data Management, Kansas City, pp. 115–124 (2010)
14. Berg, M., Kreveld, M., Overmars, M., Schwarzkopf, O.: Computational Geometry: Algorithms and Applications, 2nd edn. Springer, Heidelberg (2000). doi:10.1007/978-3-540-77974-2
15. Leskovec, J., Lang, K., Dasgupta, A., Mahoney, M.: Community structure in large networks: natural cluster sizes and the absence of large well-defined clusters. Internet Math. 6(1), 29–123 (2009)
16. Real Datasets for Spatial Databases: Road Networks and Points of Interest [DB/OL]. http://www.cs.fsu.edu/~lifeifei/SpatialDataset.htm
17. Erwig, M., Hagen, F.: The graph Voronoi diagram with applications. J. Networks **36**(3), 156–163 (2000)
18. Hashem, T., Kulik, L., Zhang, R.: Privacy preserving group nearest neighbor queries. In: Proceedings of the 13th International Conference on Extending Database Technology, Lausanne, pp. 489–500 (2010)
19. Zhang, B., Jiang, T., Bao, Z.F., Wong, C.-W., Chen, L.: Monochromatic and bichromatic reverse top-k group nearest neighbor queries. J. Expert Syst. Appl. **53**, 57–74 (2016)

Comparison Analysis of Overt and Covert Mental Stimuli of Brain Signal for Person Identification

Md Wasiur Rahman$^{(\boxtimes)}$ and Marina Gavrilova

Department of Computer Science, University of Calgary, Calgary, AB, Canada
{mdwasiur.rahman, mgavrilo}@ucalgary.ca

Abstract. Cybersecurity is an important and challenging issue faced by the governments, financial institutions and ordinary citizens alike. Secure identification is needed for accessing confidential personal information, online bank transactions, people's social networks etc. Brain signal electroencephalogram (EEG) can play a vital role in ensuring security as it is non-vulnerable and very difficult to forge. In this article, we develop an EEG based biometric security system. The purpose of this research is to find the relationship between thinking capability and person identification accuracy by comparison analyzing of overt and covert mental stimuli of brain signal. The Discrete Wavelet Transform (DWT) is used to extract different significant features which separate Alpha, Beta and Theta band of frequencies of the EEG signal. Extracted EEG features of different bands and their combinations such as alpha-beta, alpha-theta, theta-beta, alpha-beta-theta are classified using an artificial neural network (ANN) trained with the back propagation (BP) algorithm. Another classifier K-nearest neighbors (KNN) is used to verify the results of this experiment. Both classification results show that alpha band has a higher convergence rate than other bands, beta and theta, for the overt EEG signal. From overt mental stimuli, we also discover that individual band provides better performance than band combination. So, we have applied Back Propagation (BP) algorithm at individual band of various features of covert mental stimuli and obtained the accuracy 73.1%, 78.1% and 74.4% for alpha, beta and theta band respectively. By comparing the analysis of overt and covert mental stimuli, the overt brain signal shows better performance. Finally, we conclude that the relationship between thinking capability and person identification accuracy is inversely proportional. The results of this study are expected to be helpful for future research by using various thinking capability brain signals based biometric approaches.

Keywords: Cybersecurity · Brain signal · Electroencephalogram (EEG) · Overt mental stimuli · The discrete wavelet transform (DWT) · Feature extraction · Classification · Artificial neural network (ANN) · Back propagation (BP) · K-nearest neighbors (KNN)

© Springer-Verlag GmbH Germany 2017
M.L. Gavrilova et al. (Eds.): Trans. on Comput. Sci. XXX, LNCS 10560, pp. 73–91, 2017.
https://doi.org/10.1007/978-3-662-56006-8_5

1 Introduction

Over the past few decades, a gamut of various techniques such as password, token, smart card and others has been utilized for the purpose of secure individual identification both on-line and off-line. Due to the lack of reliability and confidentiality in traditional methods, use of biometric traits has increased dramatically, including for cyber security purposes. Biometrics refers to the identification of a person based on his/her physical and behavioral characteristics, which are unique and measurable [1]. Physiological biometric includes parts of the body (face, fingerprint, and iris) and behavioral biometric includes behavior characteristics (gait, voice, signature, and keystrokes) [2]. The limitation is that these are unique features for a person identification, but not confidential nor secret to an individual. These identifiers can be affected by the spoof attack easily. The face can be copied using a photograph, voice can be recorded using voice recording, fingerprint can be faked by making the mold of plastic in a hot water. Recently in Malaysia, it has been reported that a violent gang chopper off the car owner's finger to get round the car's hi-tech security system [3]. Another major problem of these biometric identifiers is verification of subject's aliveness. One of the recently emerged novel biometric identifiers is electroencephalogram (EEG) that plays a vital role as it is non-vulnerable in the case of a spoof attack and verification of aliveness [4].

EEG represents brain electrical activities graphically. The electrical activities of the brain are recorded by placing the electrodes on the scalp. Recording of brain wave EEG is noninvasive and painless. This brainwave pattern is related to subject's genetic information which is also unique to an individual [5]. The brain signal is also very stable [6]. Therefore, using EEG as a biometric identifier is more reliable and secure. For considering any feature as biometric identifier it requires four characteristics, such as Universality, Uniqueness, Collectability and Permanence. Recent research shows that EEG has those characteristics [7, 8].

EEG has certain frequency bands. These bands are distinguished by their different frequency ranges [9]: alpha wave varies from 8 to 13 Hz and 30–50 μV amplitude, theta wave varies between 4 Hz to 7 Hz and its amplitude generally more than 20 μV. For beta wave, the frequencies vary within the range of 13 Hz to 30 Hz, and usually have a low voltage between 5–30 μV. Each band has dominant mental activities such as alpha wave is more dominant in resting state eye close condition, beta wave of EEG signal generally related to dynamic thinking, concentration and theta wave usually dominant in depression, inattentiveness state. For this characteristic, EEG signal is used in numerous researches such as brain computer interface (BCI) activity [10–12], prediction of human cognitive [13] and human emotion state recognition [14]. In this study, we have also utilized this band characteristic of EEG signal for person identification purpose. Actually, our goal is to find the relationship between persons' thinking capability and identification accuracy by analyzing overt and covert mental stimuli brain signal using various bands or band combinations. This work is extended version of our previous work in which we had used overt mental stimuli of brain signal for person identification using various bands and their combinations [15].

This work is organized as follows: the next section gives a short overview of related work for person identification using EEG. We then introduce our proposed methodology for person identification using overt and covert mental stimuli EEG signal in Sect. 3. In Sect. 4, we have presented the result of our work. Finally, Sect. 5 has the conclusion for this work.

2 Review on EEG Based Biometric Indexes

EEG is one of the emerging biometric identifiers. Existing approaches show that the methodological flow of using EEG as a biometric feature can be categorized into the following steps: EEG acquisition, preprocessing, feature extraction and classification.

The preprocessing stage seeks to mitigate the impacts of artifacts because collecting of EEG signal is noisy. Noise can be generated from the movement of the electrodes or person due to environmental effect. The preprocessing can be done through various filtering techniques, independent component analysis (ICA) or common reference removal [16]. In this work, wavelet transform is working both as a preprocessing step and band separations of EEG signal because wavelet transform is a combination of low and half pass filters.

The feature extraction and classification steps are closely related to each other. Autoregressive (AR) model parameter is a widely employed feature extraction technique. For instance, Paranjape et al. [17] used autoregressive (AR) modeling with the combination of discriminant analysis and achieved an accuracy rate between 49 to 85%. Ashby et al. [18] also used AR model parameters, but they combined AR parameters with others parameters such as power spectral density (PSD), spectral power (SP), interhemispheric power difference (IHPD) and interhemispheric channel linear complexity (IHLC). The researchers obtained the false rejection rate (FRR) of 2.4% to 5.1% and the false acceptance rate (FAR) of 0.7% to 1.1% by using support vector machine (SVM) as a classifier. SVM is one of the commonly employed classifiers for EEG signal due to its superior nonlinear classification capability. Similar studies have been done using SVM [19, 20] or using SVM variants like Gaussian kernel SVM [21]. De Vico Fellani et al. [22] used PSD as feature and used naive base and k-fold cross validation as classifiers and obtained the classification rate of 78% during eye open resting state.

The neural network and multi-modal feature fusion are other powerful classification techniques for biometric application [23–25]. At the earlier stage, researchers used linear vector quantizer (LVQ). Poulos et al. [26] used AR parameters for feature extraction on alpha band of EEG signal and LVQ NN as a classifier. They tested 75 people and obtained accuracy around 72% to 84%. Recently, researchers have used feedforward back propagation (BP) neural network as a classifier. Hema et al. [27] applied BP algorithm on 15 people EEG signals and obtained 78.6% accuracy for single trail. Jian-Feng HU [28] also used Back Propagation (BP) NN and ARMA (Auto-Regressive and Moving Average) model as feature extraction. They obtained accuracy around 75 to 85%. We also use the BP algorithm for classification purpose because it is a nonlinear technique and easy to implement on non-stationary EEG signal.

In 2015 Qiong Gui et al. [29] used four different mental stimuli of EEG signals for person identification using two classifiers as Euclidean distance and dynamic timewrapping (DTW) method. They found that OZ is the best channel for person identification. The classification rate of Oz channel was 78% for Euclidean distance and 67.17% for DTW method. Various types of researches has been done using EEG as person identification such as varying number of channels, finding the best channel [29] etc. No work has been done to find the relationship between person identification accuracy and persons' thinking capability by using brain signal. So, in our work we find out this relationship by using less thinking capability overt EEG and deep thinking capability covert EEG signal.

3   Proposed Methodology

The purpose of this study is to find the relationship between persons' thinking capability and person identification accuracy by analyzing overt and covert mental stimuli brain signal. We have used discrete wavelet transform to separate individual band in order to compute the various features for the bands. Finally, various extracted features of individual band or band combinations are used as input of classifier to identify the person. In this work, we have used two types of classifier. One is ANN trained with back propagation (BP) algorithm and another is K-nearest neighbors (KNN). The block diagram of our proposed methodology is shown in Fig. 1.

3.1   Feature Extraction

Feature extraction is a technique to transform the input data to a set of features. There are various ways to extract the features for the EEG signal. This can be classified as three categories: time domain feature extraction, frequency domain feature extraction, time-frequency domain feature extraction. Autoregressive Model (AR) is the time domain feature. The statistical features are also known as time domain features. Such as the mean absolute value, median, variance, slops sign changes, waveform length etc. Fourier Transform is used to analyze the frequency domain feature. Power Spectral Density (PSD) is one of the Fourier transform feature. Wavelet Transform is used to represent the signal into time-frequency domain. The capability of time-frequency domain analysis of wavelet transform can be useful to separate the alpha, beta and theta band and consequently to extract important features.

The wavelet transform is a technique of splitting up the signal in scaled and shifted form of the original wavelet. Wavelet is a small waveform which has effectively brief duration and average value is zero [30]. So, it represents the time-frequency component of the signal in different scales and resolution. The scale of the signal can be obtained up and down sampling operations. On the other hand, the resolution of the signal can be obtained from the filtering operation.

As a result, the discrete wavelet transform (DWT) is a combination of successive low pass and high pass filters at discrete time domain. The algorithm is shown in Fig. 2 and it also known as a Mallat algorithm [30]. In Fig. 2 x[n] is the input signal which simultaneously passes through a high pass filter and a low pass filter. The impulse

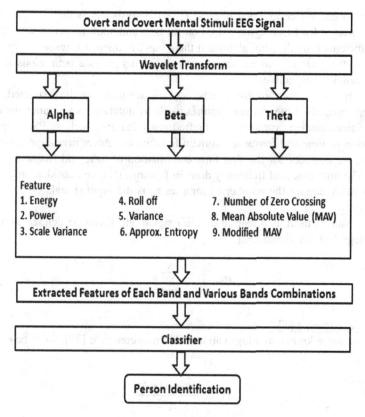

Fig. 1. Block diagram of proposed methodology

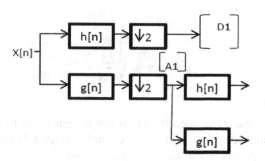

Fig. 2. Wavelet decomposition tree [28]

response of the high pass filter is h[n] and the low pass filter is g[n]. The output of the high and low pass filter provides the detail and approximate coefficient respectively.

We can separate the various bands of EEG signal using the Mallat algorithm of discrete wavelet transform. For wavelet decomposition, we have used db4 wavelet of levels four to six. We choose db4 because recent analysis shows that db4 provides the best performance for EEG signal [31]. Fourth, fifth and sixth levels of wavelet transform coefficients provide beta, alpha and theta band frequencies, respectively. Fourth, fifth and sixth levels of wavelet transform coefficients provide beta, alpha and theta band frequencies, respectively.

After separating each of the bands, various features can be extracted. Earlier researchers used the time domain features such as autoregressive parameters, mean absolute value, median, variance etc. or frequency features such as PSD separately. Combination of time and frequency domain features was never investigated before. In this study, we consider for the first time combination of time and frequency domain features. The nine time and frequency domain features, that we consider, are presented below. Here, N defines the number of samples x_n is the input signal.

1. *Energy:*
Energy can be used as a feature of EEG signal and it can be defined as a simple square integral of the signal [32].

$$Energy = \sum_{n=1}^{N} |x_n^2| \tag{1}$$

2. *Scale Variance (SV):*
Scale variance known as a log- variance. With reference to [32], it can be expressed as-

$$SV = \frac{\log(\text{var}(x_n))}{\log 2} \tag{2}$$

3. *Power:*
Power can also be used as a feature of EEG signals. With reference to [32], it can be expressed as-

$$Power = \sqrt{\frac{\sum_{n=1}^{N} x_n}{N}} \tag{3}$$

4. *Roll off:*
Roll off is a frequency domain feature. It can be defined as the frequency below which 85% magnitude distribution of the spectrum is incensed. With reference to [32], it is a measure of spectral shape which can be expressed as-

$$R = 0.85 \times \sum_{n=1}^{n/2} |x_n| \tag{4}$$

5. *Variance:*
Variance is a time domain feature. It defines the how far the various components of the signal spread out. It can be calculated by the mean value of the square of the deviation of the signal. However, mean value of EEG signal is approximately zero. With reference to [32], we can calculate the variance of EEG signal by using the below equation.

$$VAR = \frac{1}{N-1} \sum_{n=1}^{N} x_n^2 \qquad (5)$$

6. *Zero Crossing:*
Zero crossing (ZC) is an approximate estimation of frequency domain properties. It defines the number of times the amplitude values of EEG signal crosses the zero y-axis. With reference to [32], it can be calculated as-

$$ZC = \sum_{n=1}^{N-1} \text{sgn}(x_n \times x_{n-1}) \cap |x_n - x_{n-1}| \qquad (6)$$

Where, $\text{sgn}(x) = \begin{cases} 1, & x \geq 0 \\ 0, & \text{Otherwise} \end{cases}$

7. *Mean Absolute Value:*
Mean Absolute Value (MAV) defines the moving average of full-wave rectified EEG. It can be calculated by taking the average of the absolute value of EEG signals.

8. *Modified Mean Absolute Value (MMAV):*
With reference to [32], MMAV is an extended version of MAV by using the weighting function w_n.

$$MMAV = \frac{1}{N} \sum_{n=1}^{N} (w_n \times |x_n|) \qquad (7)$$

Where, $w_n = \begin{cases} 1, & 0.25N \leq n \leq 0.75N \\ 0.5, & \text{otherwise} \end{cases}$

9. *Approximate Entropy (ApEn):*
Approximate entropy is a measure of regularity or randomness [33]. A high value of ApEn defines the degree of randomness; on the contrary, low value defines the degree of regularity. We can use the ApEn to characterize the EEG signal.

Let's consider, N data points form a time series signal $u(1), u(2), u(3), \ldots, u(N)$. One should follow these steps to compute ApEn [33]:

I. The time series signal $u(1), u(2), u(3), \ldots, u(N)$ is equally spaced. So, form a sequence of vector $x(1), x(2), x(3), \ldots, x(N-m+1)$ in R^m. Here, R defines the real number and m is an integer and which is also known as the length of compared run of data.

II. In m dimensional space for real number we can define:

$$x(i) = [u(i), u(i+1), u(i+2), \ldots, u(i+m-1)] \qquad (8)$$

III. Distance between two vectors $x(i)$ and $x(j)$ can be represented as $d[x(i), x(j)]$. The maximum distance between these vectors is a scalar component and can be represented as:

$$d[x(i), x(j)] = \max_{k=1,2,\ldots,m}(u(i+k-1) - u(j+k-1)) \tag{9}$$

IV. Using the sequence vector for each $1 \leq i \leq N - m + 1$; we can construct $C_r^m(i)$ where r represents positive real number and also known as filtering level.

$$C_r^m(i) = \frac{d[x(i), x(j)] \leq r}{N - m + 1} \tag{10}$$

V. Calculate the logarithm of each $C_r^m(i)$ and we can define,

$$\Phi^m(r) = \frac{1}{N - m + 1} \cdot \sum_{i=1}^{N-m-1} \log\left(C_r^m(i)\right) \tag{11}$$

VI. Finally, ApEn can be obtained by the following formula:

$$APEN = \Phi^m(r) - \Phi^{m+1}(r) \tag{12}$$

3.2   Classification

Artificial neural networks are computing systems that consist of a large number of elements (nodes). Each node is interrelated and connected with other nodes. The structure and operation of ANN are also similar to the biological neural system [34]. So, the learning mechanism of an ANN is executed by the training algorithm based on the learning mechanisms of biological neurons. There are various types of neural networks based on the way how learning mechanism is implemented. In this paper, we have considered feed forward back propagation neural network.

A feed forward back propagation neural network consists of a number of simple neurons. These neurons work as a processing unit. Every unit is connected with all the units in the previous layer. But, these connections are not all equal. Each connection has a different weight. A BP network consists of two or more layers. Input layer takes the input features for the solution and output layer decides the solution of the problem. Another layer is hidden processing layer which is used to define the nonlinearity and complexity of the problem. So, selection of proper number of hidden layers is a vital task to get the solution for desired problem.

In this work, we have considered 9 features for classification. So, the neural network is designed with 9 features of each band or band's combination as input nodes train dataset and one output node. The network is trained by using the parameters of a gradient descent algorithm. Mean Square Error (MSE) is used as performance specified parameter and the training is stopped when the MSE between the network outputs and the targets is lesser than or equal to 0.0000001. The learning rate is constant at 0.05. The number of training epochs was also fixed uniformly at 10000.

The K - nearest neighbors algorithm is one of the good candidates for classification purposes. The basic concept of this classifier algorithm is to compare the distance between the training feature samples and the testing samples. The testing tends to find the K nearest samples in the training feature and the decision is made by the voting scheme within the training samples. If the value of K is 1 then it is considered simple nearest neighbor's classifier [35]. In this article, we have considered KNN algorithm at level 3 on various extracted features at each band and at various bands combinations. Here, level 3 is considered because at this level the result becomes stable. We have also considered the Euclidean distance to find the nearest neighbor in this algorithm.

4   Experimentation

We have collected overt mental stimuli EEG dataset. For the overt paradigm, cues are organized in a 6 × 6 matrix and each cue consists of 6 characters. Each character is visible on the screen and separated from the others. A cue has appeared on the screen randomly for each person. A person has to identify the cue from the given clues. For the covert paradigm, a cue of six characters is presented at the vertices of the hexagon. Each character is separated by $0.9°$ angular distance from a center point which is marked with a cross notation. Then another cue of six characters is presented. Total six cues of 36 characters are presented twice. Each cue is presented less than 500 ms for each term. Each row or column of the screen represents each cue. Each Person has to identify the correct cue from the screen by using his/her covert stimuli operation. Data is collected from ten healthy persons. All the person are females and their mean age is 26.8 ± 5.8. EEG is collected using 16 electrodes by placing them on the left, right and central scalp. The order of the electrode is Fz, FCz, Cz, CPz, Pz, Oz, F3, F4, C3, C4, CP3, CP4, P3, P4, PO7, PO8. The sample frequency of the EEG dataset is 256 Hz. The EEG dataset chosen for experimentation is publicly available EEG dataset [36]. We have considered overt and covert mental stimuli of brain signal for finding the relationship between thinking capability and person identification accuracy because covert mental stimuli relate to deep thinking capability brain signal and overt is less thinking capability brain signal than covert. Figure 3 shows the collection of overt and covert paradigm datasets.

Figure 4 represents the original overt signal for person 1 in channel PO8. We have considered 3200 samples of each channel for a person. The X axis of this figure is the time period and the Y axis represents the amplitude of the EEG signal. EEG signal is a non-stationary signal. So, Fig. 4 also represents the non-stationary overt EEG signal of person 1.

Figure 5 represents the alpha, beta, theta band of person 1 overt EEG signal in channel PO8. In this figure, the X axis represents the number of samples which is 3200 samples and Y axis defines the amplitude.

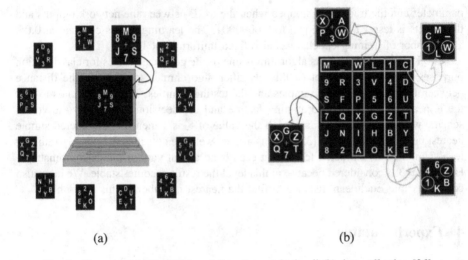

(a)   (b)

Fig. 3. Over mental stimuli (a) and Covert mental stimuli (b) data collection [36]

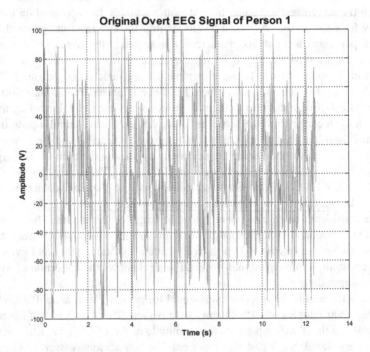

Fig. 4. Overt EEG signal of person 1 in channel PO8

Table 1 represents the number correct and false classification of each person in alpha, beta and theta band overt EEG signal. We use 16 channel output of each person as samples. So, each person consists of 16 samples.

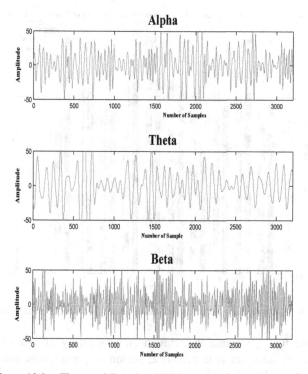

Fig. 5. Overt Alpha, Theta and Beta band EEG signal of person 1 in channel PO8

Table 1. Number of correct and false classification of each person Overt EEG signal

Overt	Theta Band		Alpha Band		Beta Band	
	No. of Classification		No. of Classification		No. of Classification	
	Correct	False	Correct	False	Correct	False
Person 1	11	5	12	4	16	0
Person 2	15	1	16	0	14	2
Person 3	11	5	12	4	14	2
Person 4	08	8	12	4	10	6
Person 5	13	3	06	10	14	2
Person 6	13	3	15	1	15	1
Person 7	16	0	16	0	09	7
Person 8	11	5	15	1	10	6
Person 9	12	4	16	0	13	3
Person 10	15	1	15	1	13	3

Figure 6 describes the classification accuracy of each person in alpha, beta, theta band using the BP algorithm. In this figure, the X axis represents the number of person and Y axis defines the accuracy of each person using Back Propagation in each band.

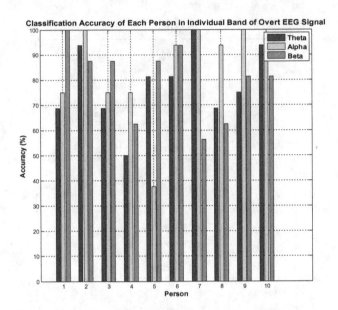

Fig. 6. Classification accuracy of each person Overt EEG in each band

From the above figure, we find that classification accuracy of alpha band is much higher or equal to other bands in person 2, person 4, person 6, person 7, person 8, person 9 and person 10.

Figure 7 describes the overall accuracy of overt EEG signal in individual band and various band combinations. The accuracy of theta, alpha and beta is 78.1%, 84.4%, 80%. The accuracy of various band combinations such as Alpha-Theta, Alpha-Beta, Beta-Theta and Alpha-Beta-Theta is 65.6%, 64.1%, 58.8%, 56.9%. We obtain the two outcomes from this figure. One is the Alpha band gives the best result for Overt EEG

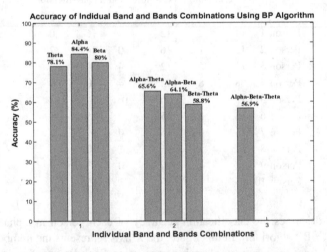

Fig. 7. Overall accuracy of Overt EEG signal using BP

signal for person identification purpose using the BP algorithm. Another important finding is a combination of various bands gives the less accuracy than the individual band accuracy.

Figure 8 represents the classification accuracy of the overt EEG signal using KNN classifier. Beforehand, we have obtained that individual band gives the better accuracy than band combination using the BP algorithm. That's why we have applied extracted features of individual band of overt mental stimuli EEG signal in KNN classifier. The accuracy of theta, alpha, and beta band using KNN at Level 3 is 40%, 50%, 40%. From this result, we again obtain that alpha is the best band for person identification in overt mental stimuli brain signal.

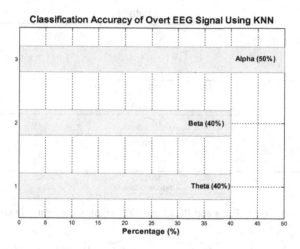

Fig. 8. Classification accuracy of Overt EEG using KNN

Figure 9 represents the original covert signal for person 1 in channel PO8. We have considered 3200 samples of each channel for a person. The X axis of this figure is the time period and the Y axis represents the amplitude of the EEG signal.

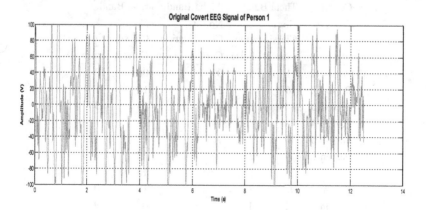

Fig. 9. Covert EEG signal of person 1 at channel PO8

Figure 10 represents the alpha, beta, theta band of person 1 covert EEG signal in channel PO8. In this figure, the X axis represents the number of samples which is 3200 samples and Y axis defines the amplitude.

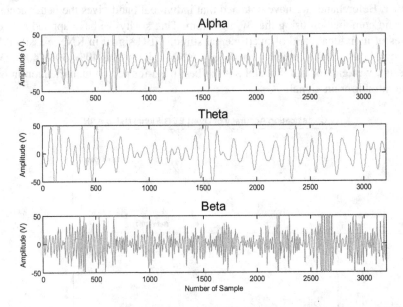

Fig. 10. Covert Alpha, Theta and Beta band EEG signal of person 1 in channel PO8

Table 2 represents the number correct and false classification of each person in alpha, beta and theta band overt EEG signal. We use 16 channel output of each person as samples. So, each person consists of 16 samples.

Table 2. Number of correct and false classification of each person covert EEG signal

Covert	Theta Band		Alpha Band		Beta Band	
	No. of Classification		No. of Classification		No. of Classification	
	Correct	False	Correct	False	Correct	False
Person 1	11	5	09	7	06	10
Person 2	16	0	15	1	16	0
Person 3	13	3	05	11	13	3
Person 4	08	8	14	2	15	1
Person 5	09	7	11	5	12	4
Person 6	14	2	15	1	12	4
Person 7	15	1	09	7	12	4
Person 8	09	7	12	4	16	0
Person 9	12	4	14	2	07	9
Person 10	12	4	13	3	16	0

Figure 11 describes the classification accuracy of each person in alpha, beta, theta band using the BP algorithm. In this figure, the X axis represents the number of person and Y axis defines the accuracy of each person using Back Propagation in each band. From the above figure, we find that classification accuracy of beta band is much higher or equal to the other band in person 2, person 3, person 4, person 5, person 8, and person 10.

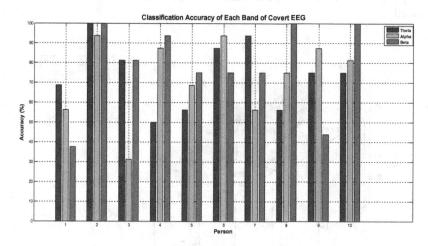

Fig. 11. Classification accuracy of each person Covert EEG in each band

For the overt paradigm, we have concluded that individual band gives better performance than band combinations. So, we have applied extracted features of individual band of covert mental stimuli EEG signal in BP algorithm. We have obtained the accuracy of alpha, beta and theta is 73.1%, 78.1% and 74.4% respectively. Figure 12 describes the overall accuracy of covert EEG signal in individual band.

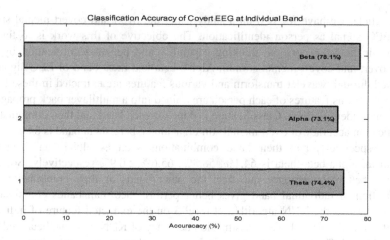

Fig. 12. Overall accuracy of Covert EEG signal in individual band

Figure 13 represents the comparison of overt and covert brain signal for person identification purpose. From this figure, we have obtained that overt EEG shows better performance than covert EEG signal. So, overt is better than covert EEG signal for person identification. From the database description, we have known that the covert database related to deep thinking capability than overt database and overt shows better accuracy than covert. So, the most important finding of this analysis is that when thinking capability is increased, classification performance of person identification is decreased.

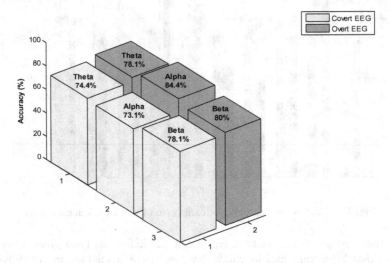

Fig. 13. Comparison of Overt and Covert brain signal for person identification

5   Conclusion

In this article, we have focused on a study using the overt and covert mental stimuli brain EEG signal as person identification. The objective of this work is to find the relationship between persons' thinking capability and person identification by ana-lyzing overt and covert mental stimuli. Alpha, beta and theta band of EEG signal are separated through wavelet transform and various features are extracted in these bands. Extracted various features of each person are trained into a multilayer back propagation algorithm to identify them. Classification is done for each band and their combinations. Classification accuracy of overt mental stimuli at alpha, beta, theta band is 84.4%, 80%, 78.1% respectively, and their band combinations such as alpha-beta, beta-theta, alpha-theta, alpha-beta-theta is 64.1%, 58.8%, 65.6%, 56.9% respectively. So, alpha band has better convergence rate than the other bands or their combinations and classification of individual band gives better performance than bands combinations. Then we applied the KNN algorithm at level 3 on the extracted feature of individual band of overt EEG signal. The classification accuracy of KNN at alpha, beta, and theta band is 50%, 40%, 40% respectively. In KNN classifier, alpha band gives the better identification rate than other bands. So, from the above results of BP and KNN classifiers, we have obtained that alpha is the best band for overt mental stimuli EEG signal. Then, various extracted features of covert mental stimuli are trained with BP algorithm at individual band because from overt paradigm we have obtained that individual band gives better performance than bands combination. We have obtained the accuracy 73.1%, 78.1% and 74.4% for alpha, beta and theta band respectively. By comparing both overt and covert individual band results, we can conclude that overt gives better performance than covert. Moreover, covert mental stimuli relates to more thinking capability than overt and overt performs better than covert for person identification. Finally, we can conclude that relationship between thinking capability and person identification accuracy is inversely proportional. That means when the thinking capability increases, then the person identification decreases. The findings of this study may act as a foundation for future research on cognitive behavior identification. Our findings demonstrate that mental activity can be used to accurately recognize a person. In the future, we will extend our research to studying another stimulus of brain signal, where a person is not doing any mental activity, and compare the results against this study outcome. We also will improve the recognition rate by considering an ensemble of classifiers for extracting more discriminating features and an advanced fusion technique to increase overall recognition accuracy.

Acknowledgement. We would like to acknowledge NSERC Discovery Grant RT731064, as well as NSERC ENGAGE and URGC for partial funding of this project. Our thanks to all the members of BTLab, Department of Computer Science, University of Calgary, Calgary, AB, Canada for providing their valuable suggestions and feedback.

References

1. Jain, K., Ross, A., Prabhakar, S.: An introduction to biometric recognition. IEEE Trans. Circuits Syst. Video Technol. **14**(1), 4–20 (2004)
2. Gavrilova, M., Monwar, M.: Multimodal Biometrics and Intelligent Image Processing for Security Systems, 350 pages. Hardcover, IGI Global (2012)
3. Kent, J.: Malaysia car thieves steal finger, BBC News, 31 March 2005. Accessed 5 May 2016
4. Singh, Y.N., Singh, S.K., Ray, A.K.: Bioelectrical signals as emerging biometrics: issues and challenges. ISRN Signal Process., vol. 2012, Article ID 712032 (2012)
5. Zúquete, A., Quintela, B., Da Silva Cunha, J.P.: Biometric authentication using brain responses to visual stimuli. In: Fred, A.L.N., Filipe, J., Gamboa, H. (eds.) BIOSIGNALS, pp. 103–112 (2010)
6. Napflin, M., Wildi, M., Sarnthein, J.: Testretest reliability of resting EEG spectra validates a statistical signature of persons. Clin. Neurophysiol. **118**(11), 2519–2524 (2007)
7. Maria, V., Blondet, R., Laszlo, S., Jin, Z.: Assessment of permanence of non-volitional EEG brainwaves as a biometric. In: International Conference on Identity, Security and Behavior Analysis (ISBA), pp. 1–6. IEEE, March 2015
8. Maiorana, E., Rocca, D., Campisi, P.: On the permanence of EEG signals for biometric recogniton. IEEE Trans. Inform. Forensics Secur. **11**(1), 163–175 (2016)
9. Sanei, S., Chambers, J.: EEG Signal Processing, 312 pages. Wiley, England (2007)

10. Arico, P., Aloise, F., Schettini, F., Salinari, S., Mattia, D., Cincotti, F.: Influence of P300 latency jitter on event related potential-based brain-computer interface performance. J. Neural Eng. **11**(3), 035008 (2014)
11. Aloise, F., Arico, P., Schettini, F., Riccio, A., Salinari, S., Mattia, D., Babiloni, F., Cincotti, F.: A Covert attention P300-based brain-computer interface: Geospell. Ergonomics **55**(5), 538–551 (2012)
12. Lim, W., Sourina, O., Wang, L.: Mind-An EEG neurofeedback multitasking game. In: International Conference on Cyberworlds (CW), pp. 169–172 (2015)
13. Liu, Y., Lim, W., Hou, X., Souriana, O., Wang, L.: Prediction of human cognitive abilities on EEG measurements. In: International Conference on Cyberworlds (CW), pp. 161–164 (2015)
14. Liu, Y., Sourina, O.: EEG databases for emotion recognition. In: International Conference on Cyberworlds (CW), pp. 302–309 (2013)
15. Rahman, M.W., Gavrilova, M.: Overt mental stimuli of brain signal for person identification. In: 15th International Conferences on CYBERWORLDS, pp. 197–203. IEEE, Chongqing, China, September 2016
16. He, C., Wang, J.: An independent component analysis (ICA) based approach for EEG person authentication. In: International Conference on Bioinformatics and Biomedical Engineering (ICBBE), pp. 1–4 (2009)
17. Paranjape, R.B., Mahovsky, J., Benedicenti, L., Koles, Z.: The electroencephalogram as a biometric. Proc. CCECE **2**, 1363–1366 (2001)
18. Ashby, C., Bhatia, A., Tenore, F., Vogelstein, J.: Low-cost electroencephalogram (EEG) based authentication. In: IEEE/EMBS 5th Conference on Neural Engineering (NER), pp. 442–445 (2011)
19. Brigham, K., Kumar, B.: Subject identification from EEG signals during imagined speech. In: 4th International Conference Biometrics: Theory Applications and Systems (BTAS), pp. 1–8 (2010)
20. Nguyen, P., Tran, D., Huang, X., Sharma, D.: A proposed feature extraction method for EEG based person identification. In: International Conference Artificial Intelligence (ICAI), pp. 1–6 (2012)
21. Yeom, S.K., Suk, H.I., Lee, S.W.: EEG-based person authentication using face stimuli. In: International Winter Workshop on Brain-Computer Interface (BCI), pp. 58–61, February 2013
22. DeVico Fellani, F., Campisi, P., Scarano, G., Maiorana, E., Forastiere, L.: Brain waves based user recognition using eye closed resting condition protocol. In: IEEE International Workshop on Information Forensics and Security (WIFS), pp. 1–6 (2011)
23. Ahmadian, K., Gavrilova, M.: A novel multi-modal biometric architecture for high-dimensional features. In: International Conference on Cyberworlds (CW), pp. 9–16 (2011)
24. Paul, P.P., Gavrilova, M.: Multimodal cancelable biometrics. In: 11th International Conference on Cognitive Informatics and Cognitive Computing (ICCI*CC), pp. 43–49. IEEE (2012)
25. Poursaberi, A., Noubari, H.A., Gavrilova, M., Yanushkevich, S.N.: Gauss–Laguerre wavelet textural feature fusion with geometrical information for facial expression identification. EURASIP J. Image Video Process. **2012**(1), 1–13 (2012)
26. Poulos, M., Rangoussi, M., Alexandris, A., Evangelou, A.: On the use of EEG features towards person identification via neural networks. Inform. Health Social Care **26**(1), 35–48 (2001)

27. Hema, C., Osman, A.A.: Single trail analysis on EEG signatures to identify individual. In: 6th International Conference on Signal Processing and its Application (CSPA), pp. 1–3 (2010)
28. Hu, J.F.: New biometric approach based on motor imagery EEG signals. In: International Conference on Future BioMedical Information Engineering, pp. 94–97. IEEE (2009)
29. Gui, Q., Jin, Z., Blondet, M.V.R., Laszlo, S., Xu, W.: Towards EEG biometrics: pattern matching approaches for user identification. In: International Conference on Identity, Security and Behavior Analysis (ISBA). IEEE (2015)
30. Mallat, S.G.: A theory for multiresolution signal decomposition: the wavelet representation. IEEE Trans. Pattern Anal. Mach. Intell. **11**, 674–692 (1989)
31. Tumari, S.Z., Suduram, R., Ahmad, A.H.: Selection of a suitable wavelet for cognitive memory using electroencephalograph signal. Sci. Res. **5**, 15–19 (2013)
32. Riheen, M.A., Rahman, M.W., Hossain, A.: Selection of proper frequency band and compatible features for left and right hand movement from EEG signal analysis. In: 16th International Conference on Computer and Information Technology (ICCIT) 2013, pp. 272–277. IEEE (2014)
33. Pincus, S.M.: Approximate entropy as a measure of system complexity. Nat. Acad. Sci. **88**, 2297–2301 (1991)
34. Haykin, S.: Neural Networks, A Comprehensive Foundation. Prentice Hall, Upper Saddle River (1999)
35. Kotsiantis, S.B., Zaharakis, I.D., Pintelas, P.E.: Machine learning: a review of classification and combining techniques. Artif. Intell. Rev. **26**, 159–190 (2006)
36. Covert and overt ERP-based Dataset. http://bnci-horizon-2020.eu/database/data-sets Accessed 14 December 2016

The Man-Machine Finger-Guessing Game Based on Cooperation Mechanism

Xiaoyan Zhou[1,2], Zhiquan Feng[1,2(✉)], Yu Qiao[1,2], Xue Fan[1,2], and Xiaohui Yang[1,2]

[1] School of Information Science and Engineering, University of Jinan, Jinan 250022, People's Republic of China
ise_fengzq@ujn.edu.cn, qqiaoyu@163.com
[2] Shandong Provincial Key Laboratory of Network-based Intelligent Computing, Jinan 250022, People's Republic of China
yand0921@163.com

Abstract. In this study, a Man-machine Finger-guessing game is designed based on the IntelliSense and Man-machine coordination mechanism of hand gesture. The image sequence is obtained by the Kinect and the human hand is extracted using segmentation and skin color modeling. The proposed SCDDF (Shape Context Density Distribution Feature), which combined DDF (Density Distribution Feature) algorithm and shape context recognition algorithm, is used to extract gesture identity. Gestures are finally identified by registering with templates in the pre-established gesture library. Furthermore, we proposed a new human-computer cooperative mechanism, including two points: (1) The virtual interface is used to control the 'Midas Touch problem'. (2) The whole game is more natural and smooth. In the aspect of gesture recognition, we combined DDF algorithm and shape context recognition algorithm, and proposed the SCDDF algorithm. The new algorithm improved recognition rate by 14.3% compared with DDF algorithm.

Keywords: IntelliSense · SCDDF · Man-machine coordination mechanism · Virtual interface

1   Introduction

The 'Rock, Scissors, Paper' game is derived from China, and then spreads to Japan, Korea and Europe with the development of Asia-Europe trade. Today, it is quite popular around world. Now, we put this traditional Chinese game into the screen with the wings of Virtual Reality and Human-Computer Interaction.

Gesture based human-computer interaction is one of the most directive ways to communicate with the machine. As we all know, real-time gesture detection is a hot topic in academic research [1]. No matter in what application of human-computer interaction, gesture recognition is essential. Now there is a trend in the research of gesture recognition at home and abroad, which is using somatosensory equipments for recognising gestures.

© Springer-Verlag GmbH Germany 2017
M.L. Gavrilova et al. (Eds.): Trans. on Comput. Sci. XXX, LNCS 10560, pp. 92–109, 2017.
https://doi.org/10.1007/978-3-662-56006-8_6

1.1   The Application of Somatosensory Equipment

Kinect [2] is a popular 3D somatosensory camera that can capture moving images in real-time and acquire depth information of the images. We can easily find a trend from the popularity in the somatosensory equipment Kinect: After the emerging of the mouse and keyboard somatosensory technology 'man-machine interaction' new era is coming [3]. Previously, various input devices greatly reduced manipulation for comfort. Somatosensory equipment Kinect application makes games no longer simply just for fun, but with more possibility. For example, there is an entertaining educational game that based on Kinect [4–6], with which students can learn to use body language. Many elderly people are struggling when using touch screen, keyboard at present. The Kinect makes elderly people experience a modern game while doing exercise due to the physical activity. Luo Zhang [7] applied Kinect motion capture technology in health care for their research group to develop the rehabilitation training system for young people. ZHU [8] uses the Kinect somatosensory camera to track human skeletal points, maps the movements range of a specific skeleton point and transfer it to a virtual mouse whose movement can be controlled by computer, which can interact with human body more naturally.

1.2   Research on Gesture Recognition

Early Recognition of gestures [9] used color cameras to capture major gesture data. GUO et al. [10] proposed a model based on outline feature hand gesture recognition method, but the algorithm needs relatively a large amount of calculation, not applicable in real-time gesture recognition. Haitham Hasan [11] proposed a method of recognizing hand gestures with neural networks, which extracts edge features from the geometrical moments of the samples and then applied the neural network to identify the gestures. However, the recognition rate of static gestures is relatively low. Yu Xu [12] proposed a system framework based on Microsoft's deep camera device sensor and capable of real-time recognition of human dynamic gestures. However this method can only identify simple dynamic gestures by trajectory. The recognition rate of complex gestures is relatively low. Marian Mihailescu [13] proposed a method that uses the space distribution features to recognize gestures under a complex background. But the identification of color images is susceptible to changes in lighting and complex backgrounds, and the depth image can effectively overcome the effects of light under the complex background. Wang Yan [14] designed gesture recognition method for dual-threshold segmentation with the depth information from Kinect. But the method can only recognize trajectories and simple slow gestures. Fast gestures cannot be identified. Tan Jipua [15] proposed a gesture recognition method based on depth information, bone information and color information to reconcile the difficulty that video-based bending fingertip recognition brought. The average recognition rate of the 12 gestures reached 97.92%, but the experiment was performed under the condition that the illumination was stable and the gesture was performed in distance from the Kinect. The recognition of the zoom gesture should be improved. Zhang [16] used Hidden Markov Model (HMM) to recognize Chinese sign language. But the real-time image recognition accuracy cannot be guaranteed if the HMM algorithm failed to establish state model for the same gesture category in the static gesture recognition based on HMM algorithm. Pu [17] and others improved the Hu moment algorithm gesture recognition method. Not only effectively solved the discrete state of Hu moment proportional change, but also maintained the translation and rotation invariance, which significantly improved the recognition rate. However, this method is only effective for simple static gestures, for dynamic gestures, recognition rate and real-time are not very good.

The above identification methods or applications based on Kinect maybe more or less have problems such as: the recognition rate is not high enough, not real-time identification, lack of man-machine coordination mechanisms, or no effective solution to the interference of nonsense gestures. In view of the above problems, we designed a Man-machine Finger-guessing game based on IntelliSense and Man-machine coordination mechanism for hand gesture. This article is organized as followings. A brief review of the related works about the framework of finger-guessing game is presented in Sect. 2. The proposed man-machine coordination mechanism is explained in Sect. 3, which includes two parts: (1) man-machine coordination algorithm; (2) the virtual interface. Section 4 is about gesture recognition algorithm, which introduced SCDDF recognition algorithm proposed in the paper. The experimental results and analysis are described in Sect. 5. Finally, conclusions and future work are summarized in Sect. 6.

2   The Framework of the Finger-Guessing Game

In this study, the proposed Kinect-based man-machine finger-guessing game follows the user-centered principle, making the users perform naturally with computer and feel fun when playing the game along with human-computer interaction. First, Kinect in front of the user will form a virtual interface. Then, with the virtual interface, the user operates the system and the fusion recognition algorithm (SCDDF) to identify three gestures: Rock (Five fingers grasp), Scissors hand (two fingers same as peace sign), Paper (five fingers release). At the same time, with human-computer coordination algorithm (Fig. 1) running through the game, the users can easily feel immersed in the game.

Figure 2 is the main interface of the game. In our method, the Kinect will automatically capture the three-dimensional position information of the hand, and build a virtual interface. While mapped into a two-dimensional screen by mapping algorithm, the hand will move up and down naturally, and the red circle icon will also move up and down to track the position of the hand in the virtual interface (if it is not in the virtual interface, the action is invalid) as shown in the Fig. 2. Then user will select the game mode according to his/her needs: five rounds and three wins, three rounds and two wins or one round and one win. When the user selects a mode, he/she only needs to move the hand forward naturally. As the user pressing a button across the air, the system will execute

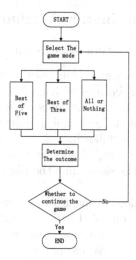

Fig. 1. The flowchart of man-machine finger-guessing game

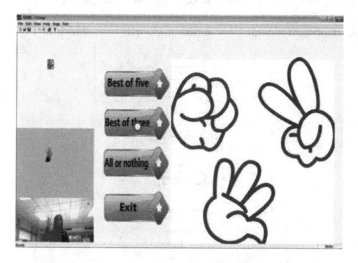

Fig. 2. A clip of our game system (Color figure online)

the selected command for the user based on the depth information generated by the gesture.

The game starts with a mode-choosing interface. When detect the user reaching out his/her hand, the computer pops up three gesture pictures of rock, scissors, or paper randomly, and determines the outcome compared with the gesture. Every time the results will be scored. When finished, the user will return to the mode-choosing interface or exit the game.

3   Man-Machine Coordination Mechanism

3.1   Man-Machine Coordination Algorithm

The key to a good game is the degree of interaction between man and machine. By researching and analyzing features of Kinect technology and related game design, we put forward the man-machine cooperation mechanism. On this basis, we designed and implemented the man-machine finger-guessing game based on Kinect. The specific steps are as following:

Step 1. The computer displays rock, scissors, and paper gestures' animation randomly and continuously. At the same time the player begins to make a finger-guessing gesture.

Step 2. When the computer detects the gesture, it will stop playing the animation, and then randomly eject one of the three gesture animations.

Step 3. The computer evaluates and scores the outcome of the game. Scoring rules: scissors > paper, rock > scissors, paper > rock ('>' means the former defeats the latter);

Step 4. Judging the victory or defeat of player and computer;

Step 5. Turn to Step 1.

The flowchart of man-machine cooperation algorithm is shown in Fig. 3:

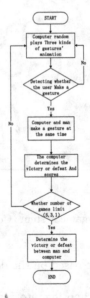

Fig. 3. The flowchart of the man-machine cooperation algorithm

3.2   Natural Interactions in the Game

There are 'Midas Touch Problems' in the gesture interaction based on vision. The user's unintentional gestures captured by the camera are recognized and will be interpreted by the computer as user commands, causing computer can not get the correct commands. In order to solve this problem and to make it easier for users to carry out the human-machine-guessing game, we creatively applied the virtual interface [18] to Man-machine Finger-guessing Game. In order to give the users a more directive perception, we put the virtual interface projection on the screen displayed in a specific interactive process. The effect of the projection is shown in Fig. 4 (the blue transparent rectangle is the virtual interface projection on the screen). The users play Man-machine Finger-guessing Game in the virtual interface. The gesture command is valid when human hand is in the virtual interface, while the gesture command is invalid when it is outside the virtual interface.

In addition, the virtual interface can be moved and refreshed according to the position of the operator's body center of gravity. When the operator moves beyond the original virtual interface coverage, the system will re-build the virtual interface based on the user's new body center of gravity. This will greatly improve the player's gaming experience by reducing the impact of location changes.

Fig. 4. Projection of the virtual interface on the screen (Color figure online)

The Construction Algorithm of Virtual Interface. In this study, we construct the algorithm in a static way: the user will naturally lift the hand and stay in the air. A few seconds later, the system will emerge around the center of the human hand and automatically establish a virtual interface. The size of the virtual interface (the value of the width and height) is obtained from prior knowledge. This method accords with human's operating habits and reduces the users' operating load and cognitive load.

This study determines whether the virtual interface needs to be moved by judging whether the operator's center of gravity is moving. The operators' body center of gravity coordinates are obtained by Kinect. The detailed steps are described below:

Step 1: Acquire the coordinate of the human hand in Kinect. In the three-dimensional space, the system continuously records 5 frames of the three-dimensional coordinates of human hands to judge whether it is relatively static. If it is static, the system records the manual center of gravity point coordinates P, and turns to Step 2, otherwise continues to judge.

Step 2: Build a virtual interface around the center of the P, and the build process ends. The value of each variable in the virtual interface can be determined by the following formulas (1):

$$\begin{cases} x_1 = P_x - \frac{L}{2} \\ x_2 = P_x + \frac{L}{2} \\ y_1 = P_y - \frac{H}{2} \\ y_2 = P_y + \frac{H}{2} \\ z_1 = P_z - \frac{W}{2} \\ z_2 = P_z + \frac{W}{2} \end{cases} \tag{1}$$

Where P_x, P_y and P_z are coordinate values of P in the x-direction, y-direction, and z-direction. L, W, and H are the values of the length, width, and height of the virtual interface obtained empirically. $x_1, x_2, y_1, y_2, z_1, z_2$ are refer to the minimum and maximum values in the x, y and z directions, respectively, in the spatial coordinate system determined by Kinect.

Step 3: After constructing the virtual interface, the system obtains the center coordinates W of the virtual interface.

$$\begin{cases} w_x = \frac{x_1 + x_2}{2} \\ w_y = \frac{y_1 + y_2}{2} \\ w_z = \frac{z_1 + z_2}{2} \end{cases} \tag{2}$$

Where w_x, w_y and w_z are the coordinates of the center of the virtual interface W in the spatial x, y and z directions, respectively.

Step 4: The system obtains the Initial center of gravity point of the human being when the virtual interface is constructed, and calculates the relative position of the center of gravity and the center of the virtual interface: $\overrightarrow{r}$.

$$\overrightarrow{r} = \overrightarrow{w} - \overrightarrow{P_1} \tag{3}$$

Step 5: Get the coordinates P_2, which is the center of gravity of each frame of human, and calculate the moving distance $d = |\overrightarrow{P_1 P_2}|$ of human body in the space.

Determine whether $d > s$ is established, where s is a constant defined in advance (the value of this article is 200). If established, it indicates the virtual interface needs to be moved. The system will calculate the center coordinate V of the virtual interface after moving according to formula (4), and then go to step 6. If the virtual interface does not need to be moved, go to step 4.

$$\overrightarrow{V} = \overrightarrow{r} + \overrightarrow{P_2} \tag{4}$$

Step 6: Update the values in the virtual interface according to the following Eq. (5).

$$
\begin{cases}
x_1 = V_x - \frac{L}{2} \\
x_2 = V_x + \frac{L}{2} \\
y_1 = V_y - \frac{H}{2} \\
y_2 = V_y + \frac{H}{2} \\
z_1 = V_z - \frac{W}{2} \\
z_2 = V_z + \frac{W}{2}
\end{cases}
\tag{5}
$$

Where V_x, V_y and V_z are the coordinates of the center of the virtual interface V in the spatial x, y and z direction, respectively.

4 Research on Gesture Recognition Algorithm

From gesture movement identities, visual gesture recognition can be divided into two categories: dynamic gesture recognition and static gesture recognition. Dynamic gestures can be defined as the movement of hand. As time passes, the shape and position of the gestures are also changing. Therefore, the recognition effect is easily affected by factors such as gesture profile, spatial-temporal position, moving speed and other factors. Static gestures can be considered as a special case of dynamic gestures at a certain point of time, and they refer to the gestures that do not change with time. The recognition effect of it is related to the outline, shape, texture and other aspects of the gesture. Because the static gesture is a state in the process of dynamic gesture change, the recognition of static gesture becomes the core work of gesture recognition. Therefore, we combine the dynamic gestures from the first frame to the last frame of the changing characteristics of dynamic gestures and split them into static gesture sequence. We improved the two static recognition methods, DDF algorithm and shape context feature algorithm, and made a fusion on the basis of improvement and proposed a new recognition method, which is introduced as following.

4.1 The Gesture Segmentation Based on Kinect

In this study, we use the Kinect-based gesture segmentation [19]. First, we use the HandGenerator class in OPENNI to obtain the depth information and position information of human hand in the images. This process extract gestures mainly by depth information and thresholds. If the depth value is in the threshold range, then we think that is the hand. Otherwise we think it is not, so that we can initially extract the hand, as shown in Fig. 5.

Sometimes there may be some problems when making the gesture segmentation that the segmented images we get are not only part of hand but also arm. So we combine RGB color space as the color model for skin color modeling of hand, the skin part is set to red and non-skin part is set to white.

As a result of the skin color model, skin color is not the same under different light. So the binary image will appear in the noise, holes and etc. In order

Fig. 5. The results of gesture segmentation

to solve this problem, we use eight neighborhood denoising methods to remove noise. Finally, we use the morphology of corrosion and expansion of the principle of the extraction to filter the hand, so that the hand can be more complete. The result is shown in Fig. 6:

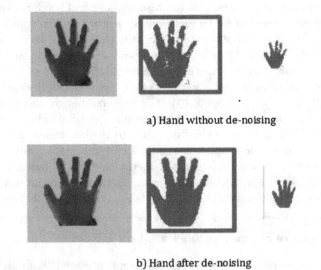

a) Hand without de-noising

b) Hand after de-noising

Fig. 6. The gesture segmentation images before and after denoising

4.2 Gesture Feature Extraction

Gesture feature extraction phase of the task is a process of obtaining the characteristics of gesture model parameters. The way to obtain the characteristic parameters can be divided into three ways: motion feature, geometric feature and skin color.

According to the method of obtaining the characteristic parameters of motion feature, the commonly used methods are motion acceleration method [20] and

method of obtaining characteristic parameters according to geometric characteristics [21]. Methods of extracting gesture features based on geometrical features
are common density distribution feature (DDF) [22,23] and shape context [24]
where DDF is based on the characteristics of extracted skin color features.

The density distribution feature is the pixel distribution information of the
image by statistically distributing the target pixel in the different region space
so as to achieve the purpose of expressing the binary image. Classifying the density distribution of the images can identify different images. The shape context
feature recognition is based on the sample points of the finger contour. The edge
points are extracted and sampled (all samples are available) to get the set of
finger contour points when pre-processing. Then, the shape information of each
point is described. The shape information is formed by all the other points with
the relative vector set representation. The general use of histogram representation of these vectors, in polar coordinates on the shape of these relative vector
context, the combination of all the points of the shape context can form the
shape of the entire gesture Context.

The disadvantage of DDF algorithm is that the recognition rate is low, especially in when similar gesture is performed. The disadvantage of the shape context recognition method is that it computes the shape context histogram for
each contour sampling point and takes a lot of time. At the same time, the size
of the contour sampling also affects the accuracy of the feature description and
the final classification effect [25]. In this study, we propose a new fusion recognition method based on the advantages and disadvantages of the two recognition
algorithms: Shape context density distribution feature (SCDDF).

4.3   Shape Context Density Distribution Feature (SCDDF)

We define an eigenvector to describe the spatial hand gesture coordinate distribution feature information:

$$SCDDF = (\overrightarrow{OM}; r_1, ..., r_M; dr_1, ..., dr_M; \theta_i) \tag{6}$$

In the formula, $\overrightarrow{OM}$ indicates the main direction of the gesture. The main direction of the gesture refers to a direction vector from the gesture center of gravity
to the farthest point of the gesture. The main purpose of the proposed direction
is to ensure the consistency of hand gesture extraction. This will solve gesture
recognition problems when the gestures are zoomed, paned and rotated.

The second eigenvector r_i represents the relative density of the target gesture
pixel in the annular region of each gesture image after the binarized hand image is
divided into M (M is 20 in this study) concentric circles. The third eigenvector,
dr_i is the result of the first-order difference between r_{i+1} and r_i in the first
vector. The forth eigenvector θ_i is the angle formed by the gesture center of
gravity pointing to the center of gravity of each finger and the direction of the
main direction of the gesture, in polar coordinates established by the principal
direction of the gesture.

The steps to extract SCDDF features are as following:

Step 1: Calculate the center of gravity point $O(\bar{x}, \bar{y})$ of the target image $f(x, y)$.

$$
\begin{cases}
\bar{x} = \frac{\sum_i \sum_j i \times f(x,y)}{\sum_i \sum_j f(x,y)} \\
\bar{y} = \frac{\sum_i \sum_j j \times f(x,y)}{\sum_i \sum_j f(x,y)}
\end{cases} \tag{7}
$$

$$
f(x, y) = \begin{cases} 1, f(x, y) \in A \\ 0, others \end{cases} \tag{8}
$$

A represents the pixel area of the gesture in the gesture image.

Step 2: Find the gesture image in the gesture center of gravity from the furthest gesture pixel M, and calculate the vector $\overrightarrow{OM}$, which is the main direction of the gesture.

Step 3: In the formula $f(x, y)$, calculate the maximum distance D_{max} from $O(\bar{x}, \bar{y})$ to the target pixel point and the minimum distance D_{min}.

Step 4: For the image $f(x, y)$, take the centroid as the center, calculate the maximum circumscribed circle of the target area with radius D_{max} and the minimum circumscribed circle of the target area with radius D_{min}. In the region of the largest circumscribed circle and the smallest circumscribed circle, the image area between the maximum circumscribed circle and the minimal circumscribed circle is separated into M subareas with the method of equidistant area partitioning (M > 0, where M is 20), as shown in Fig. 7.

Step 5: Count each sub-image area separately. Calculate the total number of target pixels $S_i (i = 1, ..., M)$ in each sub-image area, and find the maximum value of S_i.

$$
S_{max} = \max_{i=i,...,M} (S_i) \tag{9}
$$

Step 5: Calculate the density distribution feature D of static combination figures:

$$
r_i = S_i / S_{max} (i = 1, ..., M) \tag{10}
$$

$$
dr_i \begin{cases} |\, r_1 - r_2 \,|, i = 1 \\ |\, 2r_i - r_{i-1} - r_{i+1} \,|, i < i < M \\ |\, r_M - r_{M-1} \,|, i = M \end{cases} \tag{11}
$$

Fig. 7. Schematic diagram of equidistant partition

The change of the gesture is mainly in the finger part and the change of the palm part is less. Therefore, the weight of the finger part can be increased appropriately for the density distribution feature of the gesture, which can effectively reduce the similarity in the feature map of different gestures and improve the recognition rate. The characteristic vectors R and D are:

$$R = (r_1, ...r_{10}, a * r_{11}, ...a * r_{15}, b * r_{16}, ...b * r_{20}) \tag{12}$$

$$D = (dr_1, ...dr_{10}, c * dr_{11}, ...c * dr_{20}) \tag{13}$$

Step 6: Take the gesture center of gravity O as the origin and the direction $\overrightarrow{OM}$ as the starting direction of the polar coordinate and establish the polar coordinates and traverse the intersections of the 14th ring (through the experiment, we found that using this ring to find the center of gravity is the most appropriate) with the target pixel of the hand gesture. Each finger or wrist with the ring can form an intersection. Figure 8 shows the center of gravity of each line of intersection, and obtains a series of center of gravity point $P(p_1, ..., p_n)$. Find the vector $\overrightarrow{OP_i}$ of these center of gravity points and gesture center of gravity O, then the last eigenvector θ_i is:

$$\theta_i = \arccos \frac{\overrightarrow{OP_i} \cdot \overrightarrow{OM}}{|\overrightarrow{OP_i}||\overrightarrow{OM}|} \tag{14}$$

Through these 6 steps, we can get what we need when extracting the characteristics of information:

$$SCDDF = (\overrightarrow{OM}; R; D; \theta) \tag{15}$$

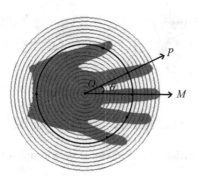

Fig. 8. The schematic of the angle between the direction vector and the main direction of the hand

4.4   The Steps of Gesture Recognition

Because it is mainly used in human-machine guessing game, the type of gesture requirements are relatively simple, mainly rock, scissors, paper three gestures.

We split the dynamic gestures into static gestures, so that the dynamic gestures can be achieved by recognizing static gestures. The gesture of the intermediate process is complex and varied. Each person's gesture has a greater difference in shape or speed, which will affect the whole gesture recognition process. Therefore, we make the three dynamic gestures simplified as: A-B1 (rock), A-B2 (scissors), and A-B3 (paper). The gesture images of the initial state and the end states of the gestures are shown in Fig. 9. Before the recognition, we need to establish a template library that stores the SCDDF feature information of each hand gesture. The specific recognition process is divided into two phases, gesture initial state recognition and final state recognition. And the recognition of each state is unified by the SCDDF method. Steps are as following:

Input: Kinect camera capture the real-time RGB image and depth of the image.

Output: Gesture recognition result.

Step 1: Combine the real-time RGB image and depth image of Kinect and segment human hand;

Step 2: Extract the target gesture from the current image frame according to the gesture segmentation method of 4.1.

Step 3: Each eigenvector in the SCDDF is extracted according to the hand gesture feature extraction method of 4.3;

Step 4: The eigenvector SCDDF obtained is compared with the eigenvector set in the template. The Euclidean distance between each eigenvector and the eigenvector in each hand gesture model is calculated. Euclidean distance of the smallest gesture set, that is, the final recognition of the gesture.

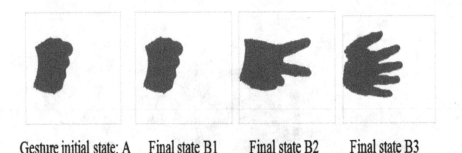

Gesture initial state: A   Final state B1   Final state B2   Final state B3

Fig. 9. The figure of initial state and end state simplified as dynamic gestures

5   Experimental Results and Analysis

5.1   The Experimental Environment

(1) Hardware Environment. Video input device: Kinect XBOX360.
Computer configuration: windows7 32-bit system, CPU is Intel Xeon W3520, frequency is 2.67 GHz, memory is 8 GB.

(2) Software Environment. C and C++ programming language was used to develop under the environment of Microsoft Visual C++ 2008, OpenCV and OpenNI library were used to process the gesture images.

5.2   The Design of Experiments

(1) Experiment 1: Comparative Experiment and Results. Because of the computational complexity, the shape context algorithm is not suitable for real-time game recognition. Table 1 shows the DDF algorithm and SCDDF algorithm for zoom gesture recognition results contrast experimental results. We measured the accuracy of hand recognition at 1 m, 1.25 m and 1.5 m from Kinect. Table 2 shows the recognition rate of the SCDDF algorithm and the DDF algorithm for the recognition effect of rotating gesture. In this set of contrast experiments, the hand distance of Kinect is 1 m. Then we rotate the hand 90° clockwise and 90° counterclockwise to do the experiments. Table 3 shows the recognition rates obtained of the translation gesture recognition effect by comparing the two recognition algorithms. In this set of contrast experiments, the hand distance of Kinect is 1 m. Then we do the experiments by placing the hand in front of the Kinect, then translate 0.5 m to the right and translate 0.5 m to the left to test the correct rate of gesture recognition respectively.

The 10 gestures, including 3 static gestures in the game and 6 similar gestures, are shown in Fig. 10. We made a total of 50 experiments, and for every experiment each gesture we test 10 times. Then the form of correct rate of every experimental situation can be obtained.

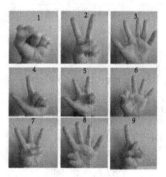

Fig. 10. Diagram of the gesture set

(2) Experiment 2: User Experience Evaluation. We set the degree of fatigue, effort, pleasure and feasibility as the four indicators to evaluate the game. Fatigue degree is the extent of fatigue that the user is in the game. Effort degree is how much effort the user in the game need to pay. Degree of pleasure is the pleasure level the user feels in the course of the game. Feasibility is the degree of viability of the game design. The lower the score of fatigue and effort or the higher the score of feasibility and pleasure is, the better the user experience is. There are 50 players who have experienced two versions of the game. Players are college students aged 20 to 25 years old. Version 1 is no virtual interface added and uses DDF algorithm. Version 2 adds virtual interface and uses SCDDF algorithm. After the experiment, we asked the players score the four evaluation indexes for the two versions of the game evaluation, the score point is between 0 and 100.

The data in Tables 1, 2 and 3 are the results of experiment 1. And the results show that the SCDDF algorithm has improved the average recognition rate by 14.3% compared with the previous DDF algorithm, and it has scale invariance, rotation invariance and translation invariance. Under the condition of stable

Table 1. Comparison of the zoom gesture with the experimental results

Gesture number	Hand Distance Kinect 1 m		Hand Distance Kinect 1.25 m		Hand Distance Kinect 1.5 m	
	DDF (%)	SCDDF (%)	DDF (%)	SCDDF (%)	DDF (%)	SCDDF (%)
1	85.6	98.7	85.3	97.7	81.4	96.7
2	78.7	97.5	82.7	98.2	82.7	98.9
3	84.4	97.4	89.0	98.9	85.4	97.5
4	81.4	95.3	79.7	96.7	76.5	98.4
5	78.7	96.5	83.5	95.6	77.8	96.5
6	82.3	94.7	83.3	97.8	81.0	96.5
7	79.8	96.6	83.6	96.0	85.1	97.6
8	83.6	96.1	87.3	97.8	83.4	96.8
9	78.9	94.3	86.5	98.6	84.5	98.3
Average	81.5	96.3	84.5	97.5	82.0	97.5

Table 2. Rotation gesture contrast test results

Gesture number	The hand upright		The hand turns 90° clockwise		The hand rotates 90° counter-clockwise	
	DDF (%)	SCDDF (%)	DDF (%)	SCDDF (%)	DDF (%)	SCDDF (%)
1	84.6	98.7	85.3	96.7	82.4	96.3
2	79.6	97.5	82.7	98.5	84.6	97.9
3	83.7	96.1	84.0	97.9	84.5	96.6
4	86.4	97.0	79.7	97.7	74.9	96.8
5	79.3	96.5	82.5	96.6	83.3	97.5
6	82.9	95.3	78.6	95.8	82.1	98.5
7	75.8	96.3	84.6	94.0	82.3	95.6
8	83.4	97.1	81.3	96.8	85.4	97.5
9	83.6	96.2	83.2	96.6	83.3	95.1
Average	82.1	96.7	82.4	96.7	82.5	96.9

Table 3. Comparisons of translation gesture results

Gesture number	Hand in front of kinect		Hand to the left translation 0.5 m		Hand to the right translation 0.5 m	
	DDF (%)	SCDDF (%)	DDF (%)	SCDDF (%)	DDF (%)	SCDDF (%)
1	83.4	96.7	88.4	97.7	83.6	97.7
2	82.3	98.2	83.4	98.5	86.4	98.4
3	84.4	94.9	82.5	99.1	83.7	97.8
4	83.2	97.7	85.4	98.0	86.4	96.9
5	82.8	95.2	79.3	97.5	79.8	97.5
6	81.0	97.4	83.1	96.3	82.5	96.3
7	83.1	96.3	81.5	95.3	77.8	96.8
8	83.4	95.8	83.1	96.5	83.4	98.1
9	81.5	96.2	83.3	96.2	82.6	96.2
Average	82.8	96.5	82.6	96.8	82.5	97.1

Table 4. User experience evaluations

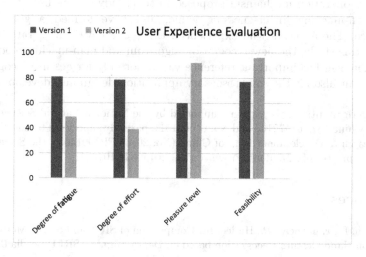

lighting conditions, it is robust. Static gesture recognition time is only 8.10 ms. According to the method of recognizing dynamic gestures in this study, the dynamic gesture recognition time is only 16.2 ms, which is very short and can be used in real-time recognition applications such as Kinect-based human-machine finger-guessing game.

After adding the virtual interface and the new recognition algorithm, the fatigue index and effort degree index were reduced by 38.1% and 39.4%, and the evaluation index of pleasure and feasibility were increased by 32% and 19% respectively. The addition of the virtual interface solves the 'Midas Touch Problem' in human-computer interaction, and avoids the interference of the invalid gesture without misunderstanding user's real command gesture, and improves the pleasure in the experience of the man-machine finger-guessing game.

6   Conclusions and Future Work

In this study, there are three innovations: (1) The Kinect-based hand detection and segmentation algorithm, combined with the advantages and disadvantages of DDF algorithm and shape context algorithm, proposed a new SCDDF algorithm. The new algorithm improves the average correctness of the nine gestures recognition rete by about 14.3%. (2) The man-machine cooperation mechanism is put forward to make the whole game process more smooth and natural. (3) In the solution based on the visual 'Midas Touch Problem', we add a virtual interface, so that the users can accurately operate the game and have more fun of man-machine finger-guessing game. The second and third points together constitute the man-machine coordination mechanism in this study.

The experimental results show that the recognition algorithm and man-machine cooperation mechanism proposed in this study can be used in Kinect-based man-machine finger-guessing game, and have formed a good game experience. The 50 users who experienced this game gave a high rate on this game. In this study, the new recognition algorithm and man-machine coordination mechanism has important reference value, not only for gesture recognition research, but also for the somatosensory application design and development.

Acknowledgments. This paper is supported by the National Natural Science Foundation of China (No. 61472163 and No. 61603151), partially supported by the National Key Research & Development Plan of China (No. 2016YFB1001403), the Science and technology project of Shandong Province (No. 2015GGX101025).

References

1. Sykora, P., Kamencay, P., Hudec, R.: Comparison of SIFT and SURF Methods for Use on Hand Gesture Recognition based on Depth Map. AASRI Procedia **9**, 19–24 (2014)
2. Yanyan, C., Zhengming, C., Xiaoqin, Z.: Gesture recognition based on Kinect and its application in virtual assembly technology. Electron. Des. Eng. **21**(10), 4–7 (2013)
3. Jie, Z.: A new generation of game revolution-a small discussion Kinect somatosensory game. Popular Lit. **22**, 300 (2011)
4. Jesús Luis-González-Ibánez, J., Wang, A.I.: Learning recycling from playing a Kinect game. Int. J. Game-Based Learn. (IJGBL) **5**(3), 25–44 (2015)
5. Boutsika, E.: Kinect in education: a proposal for children with autism. Procedia Comput. Sci. **27**, 123–129 (2014)
6. Lin, J., Sun, Q., Li, G., He, Y.: SnapBlocks: a snapping interface for assembling toy blocks with XBOX Kinect. Multimedia Tools Appl. **73**(3), 2009–2032 (2014)
7. Zhang, L., Haibo, T., Xiaofeng, L., He, Z.: Application of Kinect motion capture technology in health care. J. Comput. Technol. Dev. **08**, 104–108 (2016)

8. Zhu, Y., Wang, X., Tang, W., Wu, T.: Three somatosensory interaction of virtual mouse based on Kinect
9. Wang, S.B., Quattoni, A., Morency, L., et al.: Hidden conditional random fields for gesture recognition. In: 2006 IEEE Computer Society Conference on Computer Vision and Pattern Recognition, vol. 2, pp. 1521–1527. IEEE (2006)
10. Guo, X., Ge, Y., Wang, L.: Classification and recognition algorithm of alphabet gesture based on shape feature. Comput. Eng. 18, 130–132 (2004)
11. Haitham, H., Abdul-Kareem, S.: Static hand gesture recognition using neural networks. Artif. Intell. Rev. 1–35 (2012)
12. Xu, Y.: Kinematic Sensor Based on the Dynamic Gesture Recognition. Southwest University (2014)
13. Mihailescu, M., Teo, Y.M.: Dynamic resource pricing on federated clouds. In: 2010 10th IEEE ACM International Conference on Cluster, Cloud and Grid Computing (CCGrid), pp. 513–517. IEEE (2010)
14. Yan, W., Qizhi, Z.: Gesture recognition based on Kinect depth information. J. Beijing Inf. Sci. Technol. Univ. 28(1), 22–26 (2013)
15. Jipu, T., Wensheng, X.: Fingerprint detection and gesture recognition based on Kinect. J. Comput. Appl. 06, 1795–1800 (2015)
16. Shilin, Z., Bo, Z.: Using HMM to sign language video retrieval. In: Proceedings of the 2nd International Conference on Computational Intelligence and Natural Computing, pp. 55–59. IEEE Computer Society, Washington D.C. (2010)
17. Xingcheng, P., Tao, W., Yi, Z.: Kinect gesture recognition based on modified Hu moment algorithm. Comput. Eng. 07, 165–172 + 180 (2016)
18. Hui, L., Zhiquan, F., Liwei, L., Zhipeng, X.: (Natural Science Edition) Journal of Zhejiang University (Engineering Science), 06, 1167–1175 (2016)
19. Fan, M.: Research on real-time gesture tracking algorithm based on cognitive behavior model library and Kinect platform. Jinan University (2014)
20. Rong, L., Ming, L.: Gesture recognition based on triaxial acceleration sensor. Comput. Eng. 37(24), 141–143 (2011)
21. Fang, Y.-K., Cheng, J., Wang, K.-Q., Lu, H.-Q.: Geometry recognition based on fast-scale spatial feature detection. J. Image Graph. 14(2), 214–220 (2009)
22. Lee, H.K., Kim, J.H.: An HMM-based threshold model approach for gesture recognition. IEEE Trans. Pattern Anal. Mach. Intell. 21(10), 961–973 (1999)
23. Zhou, X., Feng, Z., Qiao, Y., et al.: The design of man-machine finger-guessing game based on the hand gesture of the IntelliSense. In: 2016 International Conference on Cyberworlds (CW), pp. 97–103. IEEE (2016)
24. Fan, W., Chen, X., Yang, J.: Analog gesture recognition based on improved shape context descriptor. Electron. Technol. 07, 1–4 (2010)
25. Gu, J., Chen, X., Yang, J.: Application of shape context descriptor based on adaptive template radius in gesture recognition. Biomed Biomed. Eng. 05, 463–468 + 485 (2009)

Author Index

Abe, Noriyuki   29

Fan, Xue   92
Feng, Zhiquan   92

Gavrilova, Marina L.   1
Gavrilova, Marina   12, 73

Mao, Xiaoyang   29

Qiao, Yu   92

Rahman, Md Wasiur   73

Si, Wen   50

Tan, Rong   50
Toyoura, Masahiro   29

Yang, Xiaohui   92

Zhou, Xiaoyan   92
Zohra, Fatema Tuz   12

Printed in the United States
By Bookmasters